TURN YOUR FANDOM INTO CASH

TURN YOUR FANDOM INTO CASH

A Geeky Guide to Turn Your Passion Into a Business

(Or at Least a Side Hustle)

CAROL PINCHEFSKY

Foreword by Jennifer Frazier, cofounder of ThinkGeek

CAREER PRESS

This edition first published in 2022 by Career Press, an imprint of
Red Wheel/Weiser, LLC
With offices at:
65 Parker Street, Suite 7
Newburyport, MA 01950
www.careerpress.com
www.redwheelweiser.com

ISBN: 978-1-63265-197-6
Library of Congress Cataloging-in-Publication Data available upon request.

Cover design by Kathryn Sky-Peck
Interior by Steve Amarillo/Urban Design LLC
Typeset in Adobe Minion Pro, Barlow, Gallicide, Comic Book, SF Comic Strip

Printed in the United States of America
IBI
10 9 8 7 6 5 4 3 2 1

For Peter, who finds what is lost

This book is a general guide on how to develop your fandom into a business and is not intended as a source of legal or financial advice. Please consult an appropriate legal, business, or financial professional for your specific needs.

CONTENTS

FOREWORD XIII

INTRODUCTION XV

Chapter 1:   YOU ALREADY HAVE WHAT IT
TAKES TO START A BUSINESS.   1

Chapter 2:   YOUR FANDOM IS SOMEONE ELSE'S INTELLECTUAL
PROPERTY: DEAL WITH IT—LEGALLY   7

Chapter 3:   THE BUSINESS OF GEEK BUSINESS.   49

Chapter 4:   SELLING YOUR WORK AND SELLING YOURSELF.   71

Chapter 5:   FUNDING YOUR BUSINESS LIKE A BOSS.   99

Chapter 6:   THE PROS AND CONS OF CONS.   129

Chapter 7:   GET A GEEKY JOB   153

Chapter 8:   LESSONS LEARNED.   175

Chapter 9:   GEEK-CENTERED WORK   185

ACKNOWLEDGMENTS

THANKS TO:

Melissa Lee Shaw, for her sharp-eyed editorial expertise

Vicki Van Ausdall, for her steely-eyed death glare

Jennifer Vineyard, for encouraging me with her words

Heather Krasna, for encouraging me with her deeds

Viki Kelly, for encouraging me with her fists

Jennifer Keishin Armstrong, for sharing her outline

Beth Nicholson, for giving me the world's greatest writing shirt

Mike Pasigan, for pointing me in the right direction

FOR LAST-MINUTE EDITS:

Iris Sloman Huff, Nikki McGeary, Jennifer McGuire, Jim Nicholson, and Mark Singer

THANKS AGAIN TO INTERVIEWEES:

Sunshine Levy, Pacita Prasarn, Daniel Myers, Willow Volante, David Pea, Laura Rosado, Amy Ostrander, Stuart Sandler, Andy Looney, Kristin Looney, Quentin Weir, Meredith Rose, Rebecca Tushnet, Katherine Trendacosta, Matt Cox, Catherine Elhoffer, David Irwin, Jon Lunn, Katie DiGiacinto, Melinda Johnson, David Vetrovec, David Erwin, Jordan Dené Ellis, Miriam "Max" Salzman, Danielle Reichman, Daniel Hodges, Joel Meadows, Reece Robbins, Troy Foreman, Oriana Leckert, Mike Schäfer, Alexandra Erin, Jennifer Wilson, David Barr Kirtley, Chris McLennan, Daniel Delgado, Greg Topalian, Russell Nohelty, Spat Oktan, Scott Wolpow, Natali Heuss, Allan Rosenberg, Mike Zhang, Cindy Khoo, John Joseph Adams, Sonia Michaels, Paul Levitz, Jennifer Frazier, Emma Lambert, Ash Miller, Tiffani Daniel, Sarah Harman, Nelson De Castro, Glenn Hauman, Peter David, Paul Charles, Jim Yelton, and Paul Mounts

Special thanks to my agent Rita Rosenkranz and my editor Michael Pye. This book was written on a 60% Glorious Modular Mechanical Keyboard.

FOREWORD

ThinkGeek was birthed in 1999, in the relatively early days of the internet, when you were more likely to have a 56k modem than a cell phone. My cofounders and I were running a dial-up internet service provider (ISP) at the time, and we were lucky enough to see the potential of celebrating fandoms by selling unique and funny merchandise. What started as programmer jokes on coffee mugs turned into a $100m+ publicly held company with lots of blood, sweat, tears; licenses with Lucasfilm, Disney, and Minecraft; and the occasional cease-and-desist (C&D) letter.

What you may not know is that the story of ThinkGeek had more twists and turns than a journey to Mordor. We sold the company early on. It went through more parent companies and board members than I can count, but we founders were lucky enough to stay on to run it for the first thirteen years of its life. Even with the support of a parent company, we had to figure out most of the details of running ThinkGeek on our own. (A parent company that sells computer hardware and software doesn't necessarily know how to sell *actual* cool stuff to nerds.) There wasn't a manual on how to run a geeky fandom-centered business back then. We made it up as we went along, and it was hard, but somehow we pulled it off.

Carol has managed to write the manual I wish we'd had back in 1999, when being a "geektrepreneur" seemed like a fantasy. She has distilled knowledge from many successful (and less than successful) geeky endeavors into an easy-to-follow instructional guide to turning your geeky passion into a real money-making business. Carol's geek-fu is strong, having written 2,000 articles about science, technology, and geek culture for SyFy.com, Geek & Sundry, *PC Gamer*, and even *Battlestar Galactica* magazine. She's also written two live-action role-playing games and several trivia contests. You will want her on your geeky trivia team. So say we all.

While I can't promise you'll experience the success (and ultimate sunsetting) that ThinkGeek had, if you have the passion and follow the advice and tips outlined in this book, you are well on your way to being a successful geektrepreneur.

Jen Frazier
ThinkGeek Cofounder
Fairfax, Virginia USA
2021

INTRODUCTION

Do you want to make money doing what you love? And do you love geek culture, the world of your favorite TV shows, movies, videogames, comics, and books? You've come to the right place. Speak, friend, and enter.

In these pages you'll find tips and advice from geeky entrepreneurs (that is, geektrepreneurs). Many of them didn't know how to start a business until they actually did it. *You can benefit from their experience.*

Learn from award-winning documentary maker Troy Foreman!

> Foreman shares what he learned by doing . . . and how he managed to get actor Lance Henriksen and producer Chris Carter into his production. [See p. 104.] It's one of the many examples in this book that shows geeks the breadth of opportunities in the geekosphere.

Learn from bracelet maker Miriam "Max" Salzman!

> Salzman's string creations became a part of their favorite TV show. Salzman's experience is evidence that even the smallest of businesses have impact. [See p. 80.]

Learn from British gamers Jon Lunn and Oliver Hulme!

> Lunn and Hulme's company Spidermind Games proves that some geeky jobs can be lucrative enough that you can quit your day job. Lunn and Hulme have earned over $1.1 million and counting from their game company . . . eventually. [See p. 28.] Lunn and Hulme will also teach you that real-world tales of geektrepreneurial experience include trials and tribulations (and if you're a *Star Trek* fan, Tribble-ations).

Starting a business sounds great. But it's a fact that only a fraction of geeky business owners make a full-time living from their passion. Many can take on their roles only because a partner has a steady job plus health insurance. Others have the privilege of living in countries that provide health insurance. Still others have second incomes.

It's also a fact that a mere 40 percent of small businesses in the U.S. make money. The U.S. Chamber of Commerce writes, "Of the remaining 60 percent, half are breaking even, and the other half are losing money" (*www.chamberofcommerce.org*). This means most of you won't earn enough to support yourself, your family, your health insurance payments, and your collectible card game habit. Oh, yeah, and one-third of small businesses fail in two years (*www.sba.gov*).

But fans can and do make money from their fandom. Knowing what's ahead may help you avoid common pitfalls, in essence lengthening the health bar of your business. *Turn Your Fandom into Cash* will help you navigate business basics and help set you up with success. From all-in career moves to a fun side hustle, the lessons here will help you sell what you make. And maybe one day, you may find your work is more than a hobby.

To paraphrase the words that gamers know so well: It's dangerous to go it alone. Take this book.

YOU ALREADY HAVE WHAT IT TAKES TO START A BUSINESS

You don't need a degree in business administration or a Scrooge McDuck–like pile of cash to become a geektrepreneur. As Glinda, the Good Witch of the North, might say, what you need to start a business is "right there with you all along."

ROLL FOR SKILL CHECK

You have a love of what you do. Business-savvy people advise, "You need to have a passion for what you do." The geektrepreneur is lucky in this regard, as you're always passionate about your fandom. At times, you may be hunched over your craft all day, comparing vendor prices at night, and organizing receipts on weekends. But because you'll be doing what you love, that passion makes the dull work a little more lively.

You have a love of learning. Geeks enjoy learning, whether it's cool trivia or a new skill.

Sunshine Levy of GinGee Girls (mugs and glassware available through Facebook) woke up one day and decided she wanted to learn how to sandblast. The people who sold her some sandblasting equipment taught her how it worked, and away she went. Now she supports her family with her work.

Even if you already know how to work leather or draw your favorite characters, learning new techniques will help you grow and evolve your craft.

You have life experience. Life experience, even tangential experience, can help you succeed in small business. Before Pacita Prasarn cofounded Tea & Absinthe (*www.teaandabsinthe.com*), she worked in retail, where she learned to arrange items in an eye-catching manner. Professional displays make her work stand out at conventions.

Willow Volante, CEO of geeky clothier Volante Design (*www.volantedesign.us*), learned about management from a job where she was managed poorly.

Every job you've had can be a stepping stone to the career you want, even if it merely informs you of the kind of job you *don't* want.

You know your market. You know your fandom inside out. That's your secret . . . you're always geeky. You may not realize it, but that means you already have a key understanding marketers hunger for: insider knowledge.

HONE YOUR SKILLS

Learning a new, marketable skill—anything from writing to woodworking to 3D modeling—is easier than ever. Thanks to online learning, you can teach yourself what you need at home, at your own pace. Find classes at

- Coursera
- Skillshare
- EdX.org
- Creative Bug
- Coursesity
- Udemy
- Creative Live

And if you're really good at your work, you can always teach others what you know.

Marketers hire trend forecasters to tell them what's cool before they invest their efforts. But you already know. A necklace of the White Tree of Gondor when you plan to walk to Mordor and back again? Yes, please. A YouTube video unearthing easter eggs in the latest *Star Wars* TV shows? This is the way. When it comes to your creations, you can trust your geeky heart.

You know fans spend money on what we love. Geeks spend money. According to *The Power of Fandom*, in research conducted by brand experience company Troika, fans invest in their fandoms, not just emotionally but financially (*www.troika.tv*). In other words, the more passionate fans are, the more we spend. And you want to give people what they love, because it's what *you* want. As *Skyrim* fans would say, you have wares if they have coin.

You have a network of friends and family. Business owners are buoyed by the help of friends and family. A spouse or parent with health insurance. A partner who is comfortable with paperwork. A buddy with the gift of gab who can help you sell your work.

> David Pea (UD Designs, motorcycle body armor) once turned part of his brother and sister-in-law's basement into his workspace.
>
> Dan Myers (Tea & Absinthe, geeky tea) benefited from a bridge loan from his parents to help repair his van.
>
> Other geektrepreneurs live with their families to trim their expenses.

WHAT YOU NEED TO KNOW

Now that you know you have what it takes to become a geektrepreneur, here's what you might not know but really should:

When to turn the geek off and the professional on. Sure, you'll be making cool things for cool people. But this means you need to meet deadlines, hit sales goals, file taxes, and pay your bills. Jedi-like discipline is required to run a business, geeky or otherwise.

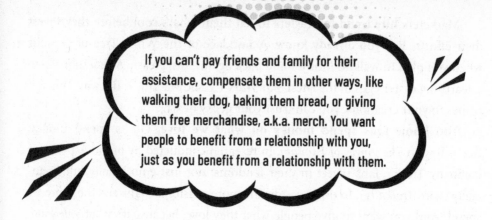

If you can't pay friends and family for their assistance, compensate them in other ways, like walking their dog, baking them bread, or giving them free merchandise, a.k.a. merch. You want people to benefit from a relationship with you, just as you benefit from a relationship with them.

The most successful geektrepreneurs know how to balance their enthusiasm for kaiju vinyl figures with keeping receipts and tracking sales figures, their unconditional love of fanfic with paying wholesalers. They know how to geek out with customers yet give them what they pay for.

How to manage money. Anyone can imagine a fabulous item or experience. But making it in a cost-effective way that can earn you cash takes careful budgeting. You may have the makings of a geektrepreneur if you

 Keep an eye on finances. Laura Rosado of Popcycled Baubles (*https:// popcycledbaubles.com*) cut airplane travel when she saw how it ate into her profits.

Minimize your expenditures. Willow Volante uses her iPhone to take credit card payments rather than pay a convention center for the use of electricity.

Maximize your resources. Amy Ostrander of The Tatterdemalion (*www. instagram.com*) uses remnants from her previous designs to make fairy skirts. "It pushes you toward zero waste too," she says.

Understand pricing. David Pea of UD Replicas learned to price his jackets so that he makes a profit yet doesn't scare customers.

The market dictates what you make. The problem of turning your art into a business is that it can end up being more business than art. You might make lovely hair clips based on your favorite characters. But if few people love a minor *X-Men* character as much as you do, you won't have many sales; if you want your business to grow, you'll just have to admire a more popular mutant.

The same is true if your fandom is niche (say, Japanese horror films of the 1950s and 1960s). If you want to earn more money, you may have to pivot to a more popular fandom (say, Japanese horror films of the 21st century). Which kind of defeats the purpose of doing what you love. But at least what you love is somewhat adjacent.

Your fandom dictates your brand. Which creates your audience. If you don't know what your brand is—the image and ideals you want to convey to your customer—you should. It's the foundation of your marketing efforts. [For more on branding, see p. 72.]

BEFORE YOU BEGIN, RESEARCH THE DESIRABILITY OF YOUR PRODUCT

Before you begin spending dozens, hundreds, or perhaps thousands of dollars building your inventory, it would be wise to first see if your item will sell. You have a few low-cost ways to determine whether or not your item may become a future product.

Make a mock-up. Does your *Outlander*-based cuff bracelet elicit positive reactions? How many? If one or two people give it a thumbs-up in passing, that's a start. If dozens of people tell you, "Send me a link so I can buy it right now," you may consider this the beginning of a beautiful small business.

Before Stuart Sandler and his son created Artovision (*https://artovision3d.com*) to sell pop-culture shadowboxes, he first had to gauge interest in his work. He created sample items and put them on the table of a colleague's pop-culture booth at conventions.

Show off your item. Post a photo of your work to Reddit, Instagram, and/or Imgur. Are you liked and shared? A lot? Have people asked you to make this item for them? Have they offered money? This is exactly how the husband-and-wife team of Volante Designs realized they had a potential business.

Start a dialogue with your potential customers. Ask potential customers straight up, "If you're serious about this, let me know." After you've gauged interest, you may find that only a handful of people want what you have to sell. In that case, it's up to you to determine how much effort you want to put into a business that won't earn you *Minecraft* emeralds (plural) . . . only emerald (singular).

STRANGE BUT TRUE: BUSINESSES CAN BE CREATED BY ACCIDENT

Creating a business "accidentally" sounds like a contradiction. Nevertheless, it's true.

• Andy Looney of Looney Labs (tabletop games, www.looneylabs.com) says, "I accidentally became a game designer" after finding he liked creating games more than he liked programming. "I never set out to do it."

• Quentin Weir of Elderwood Academy (gaming accouterments, www.elderwoodacademy.com) says, "Elderwood Academy kind of happened by accident. I don't think we ever had a moment where we said, 'Let's found a company.'"

• Spat Oktan "fell into" running conventions "by accident."

Geeky small-business owners created their jobs because they loved it, and earning money was more a side quest than a main mission. But once they finally realized they had a business, they leaned into it.

And now that you know you have the basis for geektrepreneurship, you can take your first step into a larger world.

YOUR FANDOM IS SOMEONE ELSE'S INTELLECTUAL PROPERTY: DEAL WITH IT—LEGALLY

Let's say you have an idea for an adorable backpack with fairy wings. You think it would sell well, so you begin pricing bag manufacturers. You—yes, you—are on your way to geek entrepreneurship.

Now let's say you have an idea for an Arrowverse T-shirt, one you think would sell well. You—yes, you—are on your way to earning soul tokens, right? Not so fast. The Arrowverse—and any other media you love—is someone else's intellectual property (IP).

What Is IP?

There are three different kinds of IP for you to consider: copyrights, trademarks, and patents. According to *Protecting Your Trademark* by the U.S. Patent and Trademark Office (USPTO):

> A trademark typically protects brand names and logos used on goods and services. A copyright protects an original artistic or literary work. A patent protects an invention. (www.uspto.gov)

When the U.S. government says IP is "protected," it means "protected from being used without permission."

BATMAN'S BASIC GUIDE TO PATENTS. TRADEMARKS. AND COPYRIGHTS

IP is protected in the U.S. in three separate categories: patents, trademarks, and copyrights.

Patents protect inventions. They're expensive to obtain—between $750 and $40,000, mostly in attorney's fees. You will need a patent only if you're creating something genuinely new and unique. If you were Batman, you could patent any number of bat-gadgets, such as power armor.

A *trademark* protects names, logos, and designs that differentiate one company's products and services from another, and it gives the trademark holder the exclusive right to use it. Batman can trademark the bat logo on his Bat-Signal. (DC Comics certainly has.)

For the most part, if you want federal protection of your intellectual property, you will want a *copyright*. Copyrights protect artistic works, such as movies, music, and writing—the building blocks of geek culture.

If Batman wanted to protect the Batusi dance, he could only do so for the entire dance. Singular dance moves, such as drawing V-shaped fingers across the eyes, are currently not protected—as anyone who has sued the videogame *Fortnite* for lifting their dance moves can tell you. (It would be up to a judge to determine if Batman is infringing on any works patented by Wayne Enterprises. . . .)

Understand a creator's point of view: if you created a work, wouldn't you want to be the one to profit from it? Wouldn't you want to have some say in how it's used? Most people do, as does the law.

CREATING YOUR OWN IP

Let's say you have an idea for a line of superheroic dolls, and each doll has a unique backstory. These stories tie into each other, creating a doll-centered universe. Congratulations. You've just created your own IP. It's really as simple as that.

Your cute little characters, your book, your play, your music—they're your intellectual property, no forms necessary. According to the FAQ posted by the U.S. Copyright Office: "Your work is under copyright protection the moment it is created and fixed in a tangible form" (*www.copyright.gov*).

But you can and should register a copyright if you intend to make money off your work. Do so *before* you monetize, to stave off copycats and other bad actors. Here's how to register your IP. Claim times range from one month to <gulp> twenty-eight.

Register a copyright:

- Go to *www.copyright.gov* to register your work via the registration portal.

- Pony up the registration fees. Expect to pay $65 or more.

- Provide the Library of Congress with two physical copies of your work within three months of publication.

- Register in other countries only when it makes business sense to do so; don't spend the money on worldwide registration fees until you have grand global visions and a plan to back them up. Kinda like a non-evil Bond villain.

As for registering a trademark or a patent, the U.S. government strongly recommends you hire a lawyer with IP experience. As the USPTO says about trademarks, "An attorney can let you know if your trademark should be available for your use and registration and decrease the possibility of you having costly legal problems by conducting a comprehensive clearance search for potentially conflicting trademarks and providing a legal opinion" (*www.uspto.gov*).

The attorney's billable hours will add to your expenses, but would you rather have a trademark/patent registered cheaply . . . or correctly?

USING SOMEONE ELSE'S IP

If you use someone else's IP for financial gain without permission, the creator may consider this an "infringement." They'll see you in court.

Infringement damages on a copyright run from $750 to $30,000 per violation—if a judge determines infringement wasn't willful. Willful infringement, that is, done with malice or bad faith, will run you $150,000 per violation . . . in addition to the cost of the lawsuit.

Oh, and if an IP holder *also* has a trademark, damages run between $1,000 to $200,000 per trademark, with statutory damages going as high as $2,000,000. That's kidney-selling money.

IP is so important to the welfare of the United States that it's written into the Constitution. Article I, Section 8, Clause 8, of the U.S. Constitution grants Congress the power "[t]o promote the progress of science and useful arts, by securing for limited times to authors and inventors the exclusive right to their respective writings and discoveries."

One important phrase in that clause is "for limited times." According to the USPTO's page on "Copyright Basics," here's how copyright protects IP:

 Any work created between 1923 and 1978 lasts the life of the author, plus 75 years.

Any work created after 1978 lasts the life of the author, plus 70 years; or for 95 years after publication; or for 120 years after creation, whichever is shorter. (See *www.uspto.gov*.)

So if someone owns a copyright in the United States, they're going to hold it for a very, very long time. And while your work is protected, so is the work of DC Comics. And Studio Ghibli. And the estate of J.R.R. Tolkien.

But—and this is important—fans can use someone else's IP (up to a point) two ways. One way is to obtain an IP license. [See p. 22.] The second way is through fair use.

WHAT IS FAIR USE?

Fair use is the limited ability to use copyrighted materials without the permission of the copyright holder. According to the United States Copyright Office, the court uses four factors to determine whether or not you can use someone's intellectual property without paying the copyright holder (*www.copyright.gov*):

Purpose and character of the use, including whether the use is of a commercial nature or is for nonprofit educational purposes: Courts look at how the party claiming fair use is using the copyrighted work, and are more likely to find that nonprofit educational and noncommercial uses are fair. This does not mean, however, that all nonprofit education and noncommercial uses are fair and all commercial uses are not fair; instead, courts will balance the purpose and character of the use against the other factors below. Additionally, "transformative" uses are more likely to be considered fair. Transformative uses are those that add something new, with a further purpose or different character, and do not substitute for the original use of the work.

Nature of the copyrighted work: This factor analyzes the degree to which the work that was used relates to the copyright's purpose of encouraging creative expression. Thus, using a more creative or imaginative work (such as a novel, movie, or song) is less likely to support a claim of a fair use than using a factual work (such as a technical article or news item). In addition, use of an unpublished work is less likely to be considered fair.

Amount and substantiality of the portion used in relation to the copyrighted work as a whole: Under this factor, courts look at both the quantity and quality of the copyrighted material that was used. If the use includes a large portion of the copyrighted work, fair use is less likely to be found; if the use employs only a small amount of copyrighted material, fair use is more likely. That said, some courts have found use of an entire work to be fair under certain circumstances. And in other contexts, using even a small amount of a copyrighted work was determined not to be fair because the selection was an important part—or the "heart"—of the work.

Effect of the use upon the potential market for or value of the copyrighted work: Here, courts review whether, and to what extent, the unlicensed use harms the existing or future market for the copyright owner's original work. In assessing this factor, courts consider whether the use is hurting the current market for the original work (for example, by displacing sales of the original) and/or whether the use could cause substantial harm if it were to become widespread.

How Can You Use Fair Use Fairly?

The following is not legal advice. Consult your own attorney.

If you want to know if your work is fair use of someone else's IP, ask yourself the following four questions, because a judge will be asking them too. Consider your answers carefully. Meredith Rose, a fan and a lawyer with Public Knowledge—a nonprofit that "promotes creativity through balanced copyright"—says, "The limits of fair use depend on the judge you get in front of you."

 What is the purpose of your work? Is it commercial or for nonprofit/educational purposes? If you're making a profit from your work, or even covering your expenses for your work, it's difficult, but not impossible, to claim fair use. If you're using the work for nonprofit/educational purposes, a judge would take it into consideration.

Is your work transformative? "The more transformative a work is, the more likely it is to be fair use," says Rebecca Tushnet, Harvard Law School professor and advocate for the nonprofit Organization for Transformative Works. "One can transform a creative work by changing its purpose, meaning, or message." For example, rap artists 2 Live Crew took the intro and the lyrics to "Pretty Woman," and spun it into a song celebrating unconventional women. A judge ruled in 2 Live Crew's favor, even though the group was making a profit.

How much of the original work are you using? The less you use, the better. But if you're broadcasting a plot twist of your favorite book on your scarf, the IP holder can argue that you're using the most important part of the work. The court may agree. Tushnet says, "One question many courts ask is whether the amount used was reasonable in light of the transformative purpose."

Will this impact the market or value of the original work? If you write a trivia book on your favorite fandom, and the IP holder has a similar trivia book, you may be out of luck.

Dos and Don'ts for Working with Unlicensed IP

Again, this is not legal advice. Consult your own attorney.

Here are some guidelines and suggestions for those who risk monetizing unlicensed IP.

This is *not* allowable by law:

The name of the property on an item that you haven't licensed. Don't place a *Star Wars* label on your goods if Disney hasn't issued you an IP license. Just don't.

Mass-produced merchandise. You're taking the market away from the copyright holder. And Rose says, "You don't want to displace the market for the official product." Because when you tell it to the judge, the judge won't like it.

Something that isn't sufficiently unique. A trivia book that pulls facts from the original material may not be sufficiently transformative. "If you're writing a trivia book that doesn't include analysis, you need to get a license for it, because you're likely not going to be seen as a transformative work," says lawyer and fan Heidi Tandy.

Satire. Parody is allowable by law. Satire is not. Why is that? Parody comments on an original work by using the work itself and would not exist without the original. Satire uses an original to poke fun at something entirely different. Satire is therefore *not* protected because it can stand alone. For example, authors Alan Katz and Chris Wrinn were determined to have infringed on Dr. Seuss's *The Cat in the Hat* when they wrote *The Cat NOT in the Hat* about the O.J. Simpson trial.

This *may* be allowable:

Hand-made, one-off, screen-accurate replicas of costumes. Rose says, "The fair use argument for making one-off costumes is that you're not doing anything that affects the market. A lot of high-end cosplay and detailed replicas are economically impractical to mass market."

Alternate versions of a costume. Steampunk, pin-up, futuristic, or fantasy versions of a costume may be considered sufficiently transformative. (See below.) But there are no precedents.

Items adapted from officially licensed fabric or materials. It's called "the first-sale doctrine." Tushnet says, "If you buy a physical copy of something, it's yours, and you can do what you want with it without the copyright owner having anything to say about it." This may or may not apply to selling a "kitbashed" item—that is, taking a modular product (model-making kits, Ikea furniture) and creating something the original producers had not intended. But there are currently no legal precedents.

This should also apply to repurposing materials, say, using comic books as a base material for decoupage shoes. Still, fans have received take-down notices from IP holders when making dresses using officially licensed fabric. Tushnet says, "An extremely aggressive copyright holder could argue that the shoes were a derivative work, and the copyright owner does have rights over derivative works. I think it would be wrong, but it's one of those interesting theoretical questions we bat around in law school." Whether or not this is legal will be decided by the first case of the fan who can afford to legally defend themselves against a well-funded IP holder with a quarrel of lawyers.

This is allowable:

Parody. Parodies are considered fair use. According to the First Amendment, a parody is considered a "distorted image" of an original work. For a good example of parody, check out Harvard Lampoon's *Bored of the Rings*, which takes *The Lord of the Rings* on a much more bawdy journey.

Transformative works. When a work is "transformative," it is based on an original work yet creates something unique. Examples of works considered transformative: collages, educational material, and recreations of scenes from the X-rated film *Deep Throat* but without the sex. (Seriously.) (See "Summaries of Fair Use Cases" at *https://fairuse.stanford.edu*.) "The more transformative you are or the more you incorporate review, criticism, commentary discussion, and education, the better you are on the fair use analysis," says Tandy.

Properties in the public domain. Consider playing in worlds that are in the public domain, that is, free from ownership. Works prior to 1923 are in the public domain; they include geeky literary perennials such as Bram Stoker's *Dracula*, Mary Wollstonecraft Shelley's *Frankenstein*, and Edgar Rice Burroughs's *A Princess of Mars*.

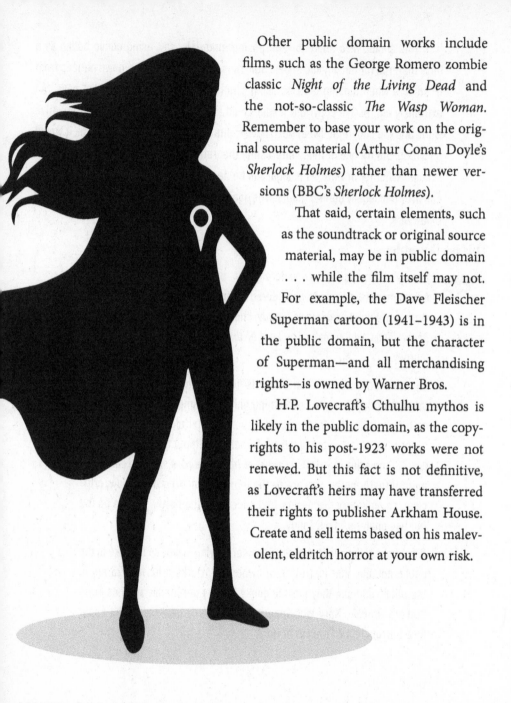

Other public domain works include films, such as the George Romero zombie classic *Night of the Living Dead* and the not-so-classic *The Wasp Woman*. Remember to base your work on the original source material (Arthur Conan Doyle's *Sherlock Holmes*) rather than newer versions (BBC's *Sherlock Holmes*).

That said, certain elements, such as the soundtrack or original source material, may be in public domain . . . while the film itself may not. For example, the Dave Fleischer Superman cartoon (1941–1943) is in the public domain, but the character of Superman—and all merchandising rights—is owned by Warner Bros.

H.P. Lovecraft's Cthulhu mythos is likely in the public domain, as the copyrights to his post-1923 works were not renewed. But this fact is not definitive, as Lovecraft's heirs may have transferred their rights to publisher Arkham House. Create and sell items based on his malevolent, eldritch horror at your own risk.

A LOOK AT LAWSUITS AGAINST FANS

There have been several lawsuits regarding fans and IP holders.

The Harry Potter Lexicon

In 2008, Warner Bros. Entertainment and author J.K. Rowling sued fan writer Steven Jan Vander Ark over his upcoming book, *The Harry Potter Lexicon*. A judge ruled, *"Lexicon appropriates too much of Rowling's creative work for its purposes as a reference guide."* (See *Warner Bros. Entertainment Inc. et al v. RDR Brooks* et al at *docs.justia.com*)

Prelude to Axanar

In 2015, CBS sued producer Alec Peters—who raised $1.1 million on Kickstarter, then paid himself and his crew—over his *Star Trek* fan film, *Prelude to Axanar*. The lawsuit ended in a settlement. Now all *Star Trek* fan films need to adhere to CBS's guidelines to prevent future legal entanglements. (To learn more about fan films, see *www.startrek.com.*)

Oh, the Places You'll Boldly Go

The estate of Dr. Seuss sued comic book publisher ComicMix, author David Gerrold, illustrator Ty Templeton, and editor Glenn Hauman for their mashup of Dr. Seuss's book *Oh, the Places You'll Go! with Star Trek*. In 2020, the U.S. Court of Appeals for the Ninth Circuit deemed it insufficiently transformative, although in 2019, the Southern District of California ruled that ComicMix had created a transformative work. At the time of writing, ComixMix plans to appeal. (To learn more, see *"'Star Trek' and Dr. Seuss Mash-Up Not Protected, Court Rules"* at *www.nytimes.com.*)

Brian Kopp Alliance Leveling Guide

In 2006, Blizzard Entertainment blocked Brian Kopp from selling a *World of Warcraft* guide to character leveling. However, Blizzard withdrew its complaint of copyright/trademark infringement, so no decision was rendered. (For more information, see *Kopp v. Vivendi Universal Games* at *www.citizen.org.*)

Avoid C&Ds with Fan Signaling

If you sell merch using the name [*Licensed Character, Licensed Show/Movie*], you're painting a womp-rat–sized target on your business. Don't spell out the name of your fandom. Signal it instead.

Examples of fan signaling:

Instead of selling	Sell this
Batman mask	Avenging detective mask
Firefly Jayne hat	Cunning hat
Harry Potter time turner	Student wizard time necklace
Star Wars' Rey drawing	Space scavenger drawing

Be aware that media companies know this trick too, and they can easily find you with a search on these fan-signaled words. Also be aware that your product's closeness to the original is an important factor. Selling "light swords" is one thing. Selling replica Ahsoka Tano lightsabers, however, is inviting a trip to the dark side of the law.

Selling unlicensed merch based on a fandom you love with all of your fannish heart will not protect you from a lawsuit if an IP holder genuinely doesn't want you to sell. Know that if you don't pivot, you risk your life savings.

C&D Notices and How to Respond

If the IP holder wants to shut down your unlicensed Super Mario Bros. pop-up bar, they may serve you a cease-and-desist (C&D) notice. This notice tells you that you have a certain amount of time to stop making and/or selling mushroom-themed snacks. Lawyer Meredith Rose says this is typically the first step in a lawsuit.

Here's what to do if you receive a C&D:

 Don't panic. Although an IP holder may decide to sue you, they may not. Still, this is the time to carefully consider your next step.

Speak with a lawyer. According to Rose, "Most of the time these things don't lead to lawsuits, but they can, and you want to make sure you're covered. Talk to someone, even if it's just reaching out to a legal aid clinic or the Electronic Frontier Foundation, which does a lot of pro bono work."

Respond. Rose says, "Write a letter that says, 'I think what I'm doing is fair use,' or say, 'I'm not making much money off this.'"

Use this as an opportunity to open a dialogue about obtaining a license. Turn your unlicensed merch into licensed products by outright asking the IP holder to collaborate. Rose says, "This means the IP holder gets a cut of the profits." And you get to continue creating. [See p. 57.]

Change the name of your merch. One Etsy clothier received a C&D over items of clothing that were named after popular geeky characters. After swapping in fan-signaled names, the Etsy maker has yet to receive a further C&D.

WAYS TO PROTECT YOURSELF FROM LAWSUITS

Again, this is not legal advice. Consult your attorney.

 Title your work carefully. As mentioned in "Avoid C&Ds with Fan Signaling," don't sell a Wonder Woman dress if you don't have a license. But you can sell an "Amazon warrior" dress. Just know that if you make a dress that's too similar to Diana Prince's wardrobe, you would still be infringing.

Offer disclaimers. Clearly state that the item you're selling is unauthorized.

Stay small. Katharine Trendacosta, associate director of policy and activism at the Electronic Frontier Foundation, says, "One of the weirdest risks of selling stuff is that success will bring attention, which could bring what you don't want. You can't be too successful if you don't want to be noticed."

Know the property you're working with. Rose says, "There are a lot of rights holders that really embrace fan works. Valve Corporation, makers of the *Half-Life* and *Portal* videogame series and of the *Steam* videogame platform, releases modding tools and sells [fan-created] mods on their store." Of course, Valve takes a cut of their profits. "On the other end of the spectrum, you have Nintendo. Its games are cultural phenomena, but the second you try to make money off of its stuff, you're going to get a crackdown."

Host your work on a public site. If the IP rights holder doesn't want you to sell your work online to, say, DeviantArt or Etsy, they may send a take-down notice to those sites first, rather than your website directly. Rose says, "A site like DeviantArt provides a level of insulation," which in turn gives you time to decide how you want to respond.

Spread your love over multiple properties. That way, your entire business won't collapse if one IP holder is more aggressive than the others.

Sell incomplete versions of your work. Sell your work unpainted or unfinished. That way, you're not as likely to be seen as reproducing original items. Plus, this gives the owner of the piece creative latitude, making the item more transformable.

Create fine art rather than commercial art. Fine art pieces, which include sculptures, paintings, and pottery, are unique, one-off pieces that have an aesthetic function. (As examples, google the works of Gabriel Dishaw and Andy Everson.)

Your favorite actor approves? That's not good enough. Let's say your favorite performer of all time has publicly praised your work. Still, this is not a license to make 10,000 units. The actor doesn't own the property. A production company does. Even if you receive permission from someone with clear ties to the IP—say, the IP holder's spouse, whom you met at a con—make sure you're dealing with the actual IP holder. (See "How to Obtain an IP License," p. 24.)

Respect the property. If you sell Harry Potter wands without an IP license, Warner Bros. will likely sectumsempra you with C&D letters. However, they could avada kedavra your business entirely if you decide to produce wands labeled with Harry Potter character names that double as sex toys. Wands that don't duplicate the look of any of the branded Harry Potter wands and don't include WB's trademarks are likely not infringing. Don't do anything that could, in the IP holder's eye, besmirch their good name. No matter how funny it is.

Understand that you may have to stop what you're doing. Tandy says, "Everything you could possibly want to do isn't necessarily non-infringing. The minute you're encroaching on the trademark owner's ability to [market] their own brand, you're running a risk. Decide if it's a risk you are willing to take." That risk means you could face a lawsuit that will hit you squarely in the bank account. So, consider starting a business that sells unique futuristic robot sculptures rather than miniature Benders from *Futurama*.

Get a license. (See p. 22.)

THE OFF-BROADWAY PLAY *PUFFS* DRAWS ON HARRY POTTER WITHOUT NAMING HARRY POTTER

Actor-turned-playwright Matt Cox wrote a play about underdog characters in a school of wizardry. Because Cox, his producers, and his director never got the rights to use IP associated with Harry Potter, "A lot of our homework early on with the play was spent making sure that what we were making was transformative enough to not break any laws," says Cox. This includes not using "official language." Instead of Hufflepuffs, Cox named his characters "Puffs."

WHAT IS AN IP LICENSE?

IP licenses are temporary agreements that allow you to produce goods based on the property of the owner. You can use your beloved characters on anything specified in your contract, from Thor's hammers to Captain Picard's Earl Grey tea.

This license to thrill, however, comes with extra expense:

 You will in most cases be required to pay a percentage of your sales to the IP holder; the more desirable the property, the higher the percentage.

If the property is extremely desirable, you may also have to pay an up-front fee.

You will be required to sell a minimum number of units, say, 10,000. And you will have to pay the IP holder its percentage for that 10,000, even if you only sell 10. This means you could lose money.

And now the good news:

 As someone new to IP licensing, you will likely find yourself working with smaller properties (see "How to Obtain an IP License," p. 40), which means a reduction in up-front fees and minimum guarantees.

Smaller properties typically don't require up-front fees, only the percentage of sales.

IP holders may help you sell your goods by placing them on their website. The fact is, many intellectual property holders want to license their IP.

This point is so important it bears repeating: *Intellectual property holders want to license their IP.*

Displaying licensed goods is advertising for the IP holder. To the fan, it may look as if you're merely wearing a licensed T-shirt. To the IP holder, you're keeping their popular hero in the public eye *and* enhancing brand awareness. Plus, merchandising also protects the IP of the owner, by demonstrating its use and value, which helps IP holders counteract infringement.

Perhaps the most important of all, licensing is easy money to IP holders. Even if a TV show is no longer in production or if a comic book has completed its run, with each sale of a licensed item, IP holders continue to earn a fee.

George Lucas certainly knew the power of the licensing agreement. Famously, *Star Wars* earned $775 million at the box office. But Lucas kept the merchandising rights to himself. As described in "The Real Force Behind 'Star Wars': How George Lucas Built an Empire," this decision earned him $100 million in 1978 and $100 million again in 1979. Merchandise for the first six *Star Wars* movies earned the writer/director $20 billion by 2013 (*www.hollywoodreporter.com*).

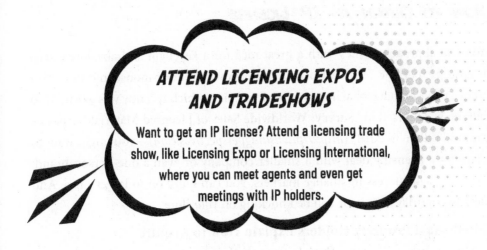

ATTEND LICENSING EXPOS AND TRADESHOWS

Want to get an IP license? Attend a licensing trade show, like Licensing Expo or Licensing International, where you can meet agents and even get meetings with IP holders.

WHY GET AN IP LICENSE?

Other than the obvious ethical reasons, acquiring an IP license has important benefits, according to Stuart Sandler, the cofounder of Artovision (videogame and pop-culture shadowboxes).

 You can run your business without fear of being shut down. Although there have been a limited number of lawsuits against fan creators, IP holders still have the law on their sides. Your only protection against the law is to work within it, as Tony Stark, who backed the Sokovia Accords, would readily tell you.

Fans want to buy licensed merchandise. Licensed merch has the best images, niftiest gear, the coolest toys. In short, IP holders give us what we want.

It may help you be more creative. Working with IP has artistic advantages: when you have access to IP, you can use characters, scenery, quotes, etc. This allows you to thoroughly flesh out your inventory.

HOW TO OBTAIN AN IP LICENSE

You can approach Disney with a great idea for a keychain and absolutely zero licensing experience. You will, of course, be shown the door/mousehole. But if you want a piece of that global licensing business pie—which recently was worth $280 billion, as reported in "Survey: Worldwide Sales of Licensed Material Surpasses US\$280 Billion in 2018" (*https://publishingperspectives.com*)—you might want to consider a licensing deal with a smaller company or even a one-person brand. With enough success in smaller markets, you can build on to larger ones. And perhaps one day a licensor will be knocking on *your* door.

Intellectual Property Holders Explain How to Acquire a Merchandise License, Part 1: Russell Brown

Russell Brown, President of Consumer Products and Promotions at Valiant Entertainment (a DMG Entertainment company; media company, *http://valiant entertainment.com*), has the following advice for people who want to obtain a merchandise license:

 Determine who owns the intellectual property. To make Official <TM> Merch, Brown says, "You contact the company that owns the IP." One place to find the right company is the U.S. Copyright Office (*cocatalog.loc.gov*). In addition, "A great source is the Licensing Letter, which is an industry publication. Another great one is our industry association, Licensing International" (*www.licensinginternational.org*).

From there, *find out the name of the licensor* and "reach out to them directly," says Brown. Larger companies will have one person dealing with soft goods (like apparel) and another for hard goods (such as collectibles), so you may have to dig around to find the right individual.

Have a distribution plan. According to Brown, "Distribution is probably the first key to having a discussion. If they don't have distribution, it will be very hard for you to break in." It's not enough that you have a great idea. You need to prove how and where you're going to reach an audience. Whether or not Brown accepts your proposal for a license with Valiant "comes down to [your] ability to place your product at retail, whether that's online or offline."

Know your business. Brown will also want to know your facts and figures, specifically, the cost of goods, margins, marketing spend, and the minimum order quantity (how many units at a minimum you plan to manufacture).

While you're at it, don't forget you need to price your item in line with the rest of the market. Don't offer a $10 iPhone case if other producers are selling them at $25 (or vice versa). The IP owners' royalty income depends on it.

Expect to pay royalties. This is what the licensing agreement is about: paying the IP holder for the right to use the IP. Brown says it's important to remember that, "while [licensing] is about the money, it's really about exposure for the brand, building momentum and building an audience."

Build a relationship. Brown says, "Developing merchandise . . . is a very collaborative process, and it really helps to build a relationship with that company. You'll be smart to pick up the phone, and get into a dialogue." Also, be the person you want to work with: responsive, helpful, and on time.

Don't assume a large company won't be interested. Brown says he never once ignored an inquiry for a merchandising license. "What's fascinating about this business," Brown says, "is that if I have a big license, you might assume that you would be deluged by people who were interested in taking that license. It's actually the reverse. Licensees just assume that we already have partners on board, so they don't bother reaching out." Even if the IP holder already has a business partner in your particular niche, their contract could be winding down. And remember: If you never ask, you'll never receive.

Don't spread yourself too thin. Brown doesn't like to work with potential licensees who have licenses with both Marvel and DC, "because I won't get any share of attention. I'd rather work with a company that makes my license more meaningful in their business." In other words, he wants to work with people who care about his company.

Be original. Don't approach an IP holder with yet another design for a T-shirt. Brown says, "We gave a start-up a license to a creator doing these very creative 3-D light boxes. I hadn't seen anything like that in the marketplace."

Create something you're good at creating. Your work needs to meet the standards of rights holders because shoddy products can bring the brand into disrepute. Brown reached a deal with cosplay-oriented clothier Elhoffer Designs because of CEO Catherine Elhoffer's talent for creating higher-end clothes. "She's in a very niche space in the business," says Brown.

Remember that developing a product takes time. Using a resin statue as an example, Brown says a sculpture, which is crafted by hand, takes multiple iterations to be created and approved. While a T-shirt can be put into production relatively quickly, it could take six months for your specific design of a resin statue to be greenlit.

If you're rejected, don't be discouraged. Brown says that you may have a good idea for a license, but perhaps your timing is wrong. "They might not be a good fit today, but they might be tomorrow." Ask for feedback as to how you can up your game from passionate amateur to pro. Then try, try again. And if your concept is transferable, perhaps you can try again with a different IP holder.

Intellectual Property Holders Explain How to Acquire a Merchandise License, Part 2: David Erwin

David Erwin, former executive creative director at DC Comics and former franchise creative lead of Hasbro's *Transformers*, plus current publisher and chief creative overlord of *Heavy Metal* magazine, has other suggestions for potential licensees, based on his experience:

Respect the brand and uphold its image. As fans of Larry Niven's 1969 tongue-in-cheek essay (and example of fair use) "Man of Steel, Woman of Kleenex" know, condoms are important to the health and well-being of any person Superman would choose to partner with.

Still, Erwin rejected a proposal for Superman-themed condoms. He specifically dismissed this because, "They did not fit within the position of what our brand represents." Superman's brand is a family-friendly one.

Meanwhile, the Batmobile is as much a part of Bat-lore as any rogue in the gallery, and a toy car fits neatly within the DC Universe's marketing plan. With this in mind, DC has licensed dozens of vehicles, including a small toy car with a missile launcher, a remote-controlled Batmobile, and even a pedaled go-kart. These items are on brand and suitable for a wide audience.

"If you don't uphold your image and really communicate what you represent, there is no brand," says Erwin.

Follow the IP holder's guidelines. When licensing *Transformers* toys, Erwin put strict guidelines in place for characters. For example, when one character is seen in profile, "he has two wheels on the lower part of his legs."

So when a plush manufacturer submitted a design with only one wheel shown in profile, Erwin rejected it. "I would insist on two wheels, because it needs to be consistent."

Fill in the IP holder's gaps. Take a look at the IP holder's product lines, and see if there are gaps in its offerings. You're an artist who doesn't see enough artwork of your favorite new TV show? You might want to reach out to its licensing division. It wouldn't hurt to offer multiple character sketches at varying price points.

IP CASE STUDIES

IP licensors won't trust just anyone with their brand. You need to prove your professionalism, and you need to show an ability to turn a profit. But there are rare occasions when the right people can start from zero and acquire an IP license. Here's how.

Case Study: Spidermind Writes a Successful IP Proposal

English gamers Jon Lunn and Oliver Hulme were chatting when the conversation turned toward their favorite 1980s' space simulation, *Elite*. The videogame had recently received a 21st-century revamp, *Elite Dangerous*. Lunn and Hulme realized that it would make an excellent role-playing game (RPG).

As it turns out, Hulme liked designing game systems for fun, and Lunn was comfortable handling business details. They formed Spidermind Games and went to work. They were, as Lunn put it, "Two blokes in a shed."

But this was no easy road to riches. All told, it took the two friends *four years* from their eureka moment to placing the RPG tomes in their customers' hands.

Spidermind's second game, a two-player card game also based on *Elite Dangerous*, had more hitches than Thanos had infinity stones. For starters, it took eighteen months for Spidermind to simply arrange a meeting with Frontier Developments, the company that created *Elite Dangerous*.

After selling the idea to Frontier and signing a contract, Lunn and Hulme went to work. While Hulme wrote the four-hundred-page guide, Lunn handled Spidermind's many logistics. Setting up a company. Hiring the artists. Buying ISBN numbers and barcodes for each of the RPG's books (and even its Games Master, or GM, screen). Pricing out game printing companies. Choosing a box manufacturer. Finding distributors. Securing a fulfillment company. All while the two of them maintained full-time jobs and raised families. That took another eighteen months.

Eventually, Lunn and Hulme created a Kickstarter to help with expenses. Their ask was £40,000 ($58,000), and they were reasonably confident their project would earn out. In fact, they soon took in a comfortable £60,000 ($85,000) . . .

And then, three days before the campaign ended, Spidermind's campaign was issued a take-down notice. According to Lunn, "A copyright troll had claimed they owned the rights to the original videogame *Elite*."

Kickstarter gave the claimant fifteen days to produce proof of ownership. When the claimant did not, "Fifteen days later, we were up and running," says Lunn. Perhaps due to the industry press the take-down received, Spidermind raised a total of £86,000 ($125,000).

When it came to fulfilling orders, snags included an accidental merging of all of the backer's mailing addresses, plus stalled backer rewards, due to an untimely death (see p. 76.).

Yet the RPG was successful enough that, in 2018, Spidermind created a Kickstarter for *Elite Dangerous: Battle Cards*, a two-player expandable card game . . . that was also pulled by Kickstarter based on a take-down request from the same claimant as before. This time, however, Kickstarter took *five months* to look into this copyright claim. In those five months, Spidermind lost customers and therefore money. It was, Lunn says, "Hugely frustrating."

But Spidermind had a surprise ally in Frontier, who provided the lawyers to kickstart the second Kickstarter. *Elite Dangerous: Battle Cards* finally made it into the hands of its backers in 2020. And the minds behind Spidermind have continued to create.

Their proposal worked for several reasons:

They had the right idea. An RPG is an obvious complement to a video-game with a deep history and lore, and with the dedicated fanbase of *Elite Dangerous*—Frontier Developments was worth $1.26 billion in 2020 ("Frontier Developments Named Business of the Year," *www.business weekly.co.uk*)—any RPG based on it has a built-in market. Also, the people who played a space-themed RPG are the types of gamers that Frontier would likely want to attract to *Elite Dangerous*.

They spoke with Frontier directly. If you're chasing an IP, find the schedule of the IP holder's upcoming conventions, conferences, and collaborative events. Lunn and Hulme approached Frontier at a convention, where they were able to acquire the contact details of the person in charge of licensing. (Even then, it took eighteen months between contacting the IP department and signing the contract.)

They wrote a professional proposal. Lunn had never written an IP proposal before, but he extrapolated what Frontier would want to see: ideas for funding, a look at the competition, and a plan for distribution. He included a realistic timeline, as well as a media plan. He rounded it out with a sample of the game. He also emphasized that this was a money-making proposition, while maintaining an awareness that Frontier Development had complete oversight on the project. See it for yourself.

Licence Application

INDEX

Introduction

What is a Role Playing Game?

Elite: The Role Playing Game

The Playtest Book—'The Worst Intentions'

Why a Kickstarter Campaign?

Back Office and Fulfilments

Pledge Levels

Suppliers

Stretch Goals

Production Timescale

Our Team

Introduction

Elite: Dangerous deserves a role playing game.

Not only do the two platforms merge seamlessly together but in the case of Elite: Dangerous (ED), more so than many computer games, it has adopted as one of its core principles the idea of the 'sandbox' approach to play. This concept of forging your own path, choosing your own destiny is the foundation on which every popular role playing game is based and is the key to its success.

Elite: The Role Playing Game (Elite: The RPG) is now at the stage where, with a licence from frontier, it is ready to launch the product on both the Elite: Dangerous community and the international role playing community.

The plan is to use Kickstarter as a month-long preorder campaign not only to sell a number of the core items and finance further purchase of stock but also to fund further expansions of the game.

- We have a play test game already written and fully designed. A 50-page PDF to be given away during the lead up to and throughout the Kickstarter Campaign. This stand-alone adventure contains the basics of the role playing game (RPG) without giving away the game mechanics in too much detail.

To download a copy of this playtest document, click here (dropbox folder)

- Following the granting of a licence, we would like to engage in a period of pre-launch PR through the various Elite Dangerous mediums bringing the game and the Kickstarter Campaign to the notice of as many players as possible. Our worldwide distributor, Modiphius Entertainment, will also conduct a full pre-launch campaign through their site and through Drivethru RPG, the world's largest RPG download store. Both sites plan to offer the playtest book for free download.

- We have set our initial pledge target level at £25,000.

- We are modelling the campaign along the lines of Modiphius who have successfully launched several RPG Games through Kickstarter, one of which was Corvus Belli's Infinity RPG Kickstarter. That campaign raised £346,330 from 3,494 backers. Infinity is a table top miniatures game invented by a group of friends in Spain in 2005. A number of the backers came from a fan base of some 8,000 subscribing Infinity players.

- Pledge levels for our Kickstarter campaign begin at £5 and continue up to £500 (Pledge list attached).

- We have included examples of some of the stretch goals included in the campaign but have many more that can be added.

- The RPG mirrors the universe of Elite: Dangerous

  ▷ Ships & their components all exist in the game and function in close correspondence with the computer game. This means that player of ED will feel at home and those new to ED will want to experience the computer game.

  ▷ The RPG is easily adaptable to the new seasons released by ED. It is the aim of the RPG to follow the events and construction of the ED world so that the two playing experiences are closely aligned.

- The game uses a version of procedural generation to aid the Games Master or story teller in creating the adventure as they go, saving time on preparation. Examples of this include:

  ▷ Stars and star systems.

  ▷ Stories and missions.

  ▷ NPC's including their statistics and their names.

- The pace is fast and fluid with simple character generation with easily recognisable skills and attributes, whilst making the character generation highly customisable like their ships.

- On top of common skills and attributes characters can choose a select number of extraordinary abilities (Karmic Capabilities) that give them an edge on performing a task or defeating an enemy. These are currently broken down in to Spaceship, Vehicle and Personal and are either defensive or offensive. Examples include:

  ▷ 'I have you now' (Spaceship attack)—Gives a bonus to Spaceship dogfighting

  ▷ Karmic missile (Spaceship attack)—Allows your missiles to temporarily ignore countermeasures

  ▷ Without even looking (Personal attack)—Allows you to engage someone standing behind you as a bonus shot without even looking at them.

> ▷ Dive aside (Personal defence)—A super dodge which adds a significant bonus to your defensive roll.

We know that one fan, who purchased one of the Kickstarter Author Packs for ED, has been developing a role playing game since 2013, but this project, Elite Encounters, is some 18 months behind schedule. Poor health, a new job and a family fast losing patience are only some of the reasons cited on the designer's update page as to why there is no game as of yet. If he does succeed then this will be celebrated as healthy competition from another passionate fan, if he doesn't then Elite still deserves an RPG.

What we would very much like to do is move away from the community based 'hobbyist' model, with hit and miss deadlines and instead, produce a professional compliment to Elite: Dangerous. We fully embrace the ideas of editorial oversight as well as revenue share from the Kickstarter onwards. We know the RPG would most definitely benefit from some exposure to the Elite community; we would also like to think that Elite Dangerous would benefit from exposure to the RPG community.

Our media plan includes attending fairs, online play testing, bombarding the forums and with a free sample given away at the beginning of the Kickstarter campaign everyone will have an opinion on the product and hopefully want to give voice to that. One excellent feature of the Infinity Kickstarter is the offering of more in game rewards for reaching targets on such things as Facebook likes and retweets.

Once fully produced and approved we would then look to market the Role Playing Game, not only with the help of Frontier to the Video Gaming community, but also through RPG platforms both here in the UK and internationally, with the hope of taking the Elite brand to a whole new audience.

Should you wish to discuss this further we would be delighted to make ourselves available for a telephone call, skype or face time meeting or equally happy to come up to Cambridge and pitch our idea and demo the game.

What is a Role Playing Game?

'A role-playing game (RPG) is a game in which players assume the roles of characters in a fictional setting. Players take responsibility for acting out these roles within a narrative, either through literal acting or through a process of structured decision-making or character development. Actions taken within many games succeed or fail according to a formal system of rules and guidelines.' (Wikipedia — Role Playing Games)

A role playing game or RPG is a table top game where, directed by a Games Master (GM), a group of players embark on a mission or adventure in a fantasy world. Whether that world is full of dragons, swords and sorcery or space battles amongst the stars, each player takes control of a character in that universe and forms, with the other players around the table, a group or band ready to head off and find adventure.

Under the watchful eye of the GM, each player is initially encouraged to create their character, often using dice to decide on attributes and skills. Once created, they join their band of fellow adventurers and embark on a journey or 'campaign' limited only by their imagination. The GM acts as the story teller, referee and the controller of the myriad of non-player characters (NPC's) that the players will encounter.

Throughout the campaign the GM uses the rules written in the RPG book to guide the actions of the players, often requiring them to roll a dice to decide the success or failure of a particular task. Players will be required to perform a variety of actions in order to successfully complete their mission or campaign, gaining valuable experience en-route. That experience is converted into opportunities for that player to advance their character, increasing their skills and attributes in readiness for the next adventure.

Elite: The Role Playing Game (from the Core Manual)

Elite: The Role Playing game (Elite: The RPG) is an interactive adventure you share with a group of friends. It is set in the universe of Elite created by David

Braben and Ian Bell, a futuristic galaxy in which spaceflight is common, amazing technology is freely available, and danger is everywhere. As a player you will own your own spacecraft and travel to fantastic locations, exploring new worlds, defeating deadly enemies and outwitting powerful opponents who will stop at nothing to destroy you.

In Elite: The RPG, each player creates their own character by selecting from a number of different backgrounds. Perhaps your character was an orphan from a corporate world where the unemployed are hunted down by the police—you survived at first on your wits and then with the help of charitable friends who gave you a place to stay and the chance for an education. Perhaps you are an ex-army grunt who's seen too many wars, or a cheerleader who fell in with the wrong crowd and is now a notorious criminal. Really anything is possible, and each background you pick increases your skills across a number of different areas.

One player becomes the Gamesmaster (GM). This is the person who tells the story, plays all the people and villains the characters meet and creates the adventure. The same person does not have to be the GM for every adventure, although oddly enough it's hard to stop once you undertake that role. In Elite: The RPG, being the GM is a little bit easier than in most role playing games as you can create many missions, encounters and maps randomly. The Random Generation System (RGS) is there to help you—and you can use it as much or as little as you like. It is a powerful tool that lets you play a game with very little preparation, but never feel that you cannot take ownership of the results. You can run a game of Elite: The RPG without using the RGS at all, and indeed, once you have the game mastered you will find that you will use it less and less.

A Galaxy of Adventure

In the universe of Elite: Dangerous? cheap and readily available faster than light travel has allowed humanity to explode across the stars, building new colonies, cities, nations and empires. The galaxy is a rich place, filled with a wealth of minerals, water and life bearing planets. The great nations of the Federation, Empire and Alliance grow wealthier every day, and such wealth attracts powerful people who scheme every day to increase their power.

Space travel is common and affordable. The middle classes of the galaxy own spaceships like twentieth-century families own cars. Owning a spaceship grants tremendous freedom—spacecraft owners are courted all across the galaxy by space stations hungry for rare goods and vital supplies. Politics seldom interferes with trade and even very patriotic worlds such as Nanomam are happy to accept goods and services from those who paint the 'wrong' flag on the side of their spacecraft.

For those at the bottom of the heap little has changed since the old Earth dark ages. Planet-spanning mega corporations rule unchecked in large parts of the galaxy employing entire nations of people in call centres, factories, tech support hubs or even as humble stockbrokers. On the planet of Zaonce the miserable masses slave for the planet wide Bank of Zaonce, filling tedious hours buying stocks and shares, selling high and low like robots, receiving none of the gains they make. In revolutionary Eranin the population are expected to perform in weekly parades celebrating their independence from the Federation, even while their leaders 'redistribute' the people's wages into their own back pockets.

This combination of cheap space travel, terrible inequality and a laissez faire attitude towards weapon ownership makes the galaxy a dangerous place. Pirates, mercenaries and political agitators often like to fire first and seldom ask questions later. The police have a terrible arrest rate, but an excellent execution record; in space it's hard to take prisoners and very few people even try. Add to this the many navigational hazards in space, fierce native creatures on unexplored planets, psychotic cyborg's with faulty behaviour chips and the terrible greed of the intergalactic elite and you have a dangerous galaxy just waiting to destroy a wandering space pilot.

To survive you're going to need the best ship, the best equipment, a strong credit account and the skills to back it all up. For in this dangerous galaxy only the elite survive ...

The Worst Intentions—A standalone adventure for Elite: The Role Playing Game

Playtest?

It is common practice for companies who intend on launching a new RPG, to first launch a free 'playtest' document prior to making the core manual available for purchase.

Whilst it is called a 'playtest' document this is something of a misnomer as it is more of a taster than a playtest as most of the core playtesting of the game would have had to have been completed before publication.

This being said we would not be insensitive to ideas from the community that might make the game easier to play.

The Synopsys (taken from the Playtest)

'The players begin as police detectives for the independent Asellus Primus system. Each player has a Viper Spaceship, a police interdiction and combat ship used to enforce law in the sector. Their ships also contain a special vehicle called a Surface Reconnaissance Vehicle (SRV) which is a little like a super-advanced moon buggy. The SRV is designed to be used on any planet, even those without atmosphere. It is basically the player's 'police car'. There are four characters to choose from—have your players pick one they like, or assign them randomly.

The game mechanics

Whilst this standalone playtest adventure is designed for a maximum of five players, the game itself will be able to handle up to 8 players and one Games Master as a maximum but it can become a little unruly beyond 6 players.

The Playtest has pre-rolled characters and ships already kitted out and as is explained in the playtest doc:

What is not included are:

- Character Creation rules
- Adventure Creation rules
- Spaceship modification rules
- Equipment lists (except the equipment listed in the game)
- The full combat rules (partial rules for this adventure are included)
- Lots and lots of other stuff

What is contained within the playtest are:

- The basics of the D10 system used in the game
- An explanation and opportunity to experience the three main combat systems:
  - Spaceship Combat
  - Personal Combat
  - Vehicle Combat
- An explanation of 'Karma Capabilities', special abilities that you[r] players can call upon in a jam.

The adventure is fairly linear with little opportunity to range too far off piste, however, there should be enough to wet the player's appetite and make the GM look forward to fleshing out the game with the full rules, Core Manual.

Why use a Kickstarter Campaign?

Many Kickstarter (KS) Projects are well meaning but Hobbyist in their nature, they also run the risk that even if they are funded, the well-meaning recipient of the money is unable to deliver.

Producing this RPG is not a hobby, it is our job. Writing for Elite: The RPG has been a full time job for Oliver for the last six months while Jon has split his time between this project and a part time self-employed job. Both have funded all aspects of the project and following the granting of the licence will become full time, dedicated staff on this project alone.

The main core book is expected to be fully written by the end of Jun[e] and the first print run will be posted by the end of August / start of September. If we were able to run our KS campaign for the month of May, this would mean that on successful funding we could send all the contributors their PDF of the core book within two months.

So Kickstarter isn't to raise some initial capital?

Although Kickstarter, as its name suggests, sees its main purpose as the place for seed funding projects, for the world of RPG's it is something of a panacea.

To continue with the stretching of metaphors, for the world of RPG, the stars are very much aligned at present due to a number of factors:

- RPG's became widely spread from the creation of Dungeons and Dragons around the mid 70's. From then on the appeal grew with the main demographic being the rather nerdy 'geek' teenager. The problem with that was the spending power of that age group meaning books were seen as expensive and 'saved up for'. Those same people are now in their 40's and many are in relatively well paid jobs.

- Geek is now cool with the Big Bang Theory as well as other popular shows and films showing the nerd as cool and mainstream. RPG's are more popular now than they have ever been. Chessex, the UK's premier dice manufacturers told us recently on a telephone call that their business is growing at a steady 20% per year.

- Back in the 70's and 80's an RPG game publisher would have to pay upfront for the printing of copies of the various books, guessing on how many they might sell. Kickstarter can take pre orders, meaning a print run only needs to be paid for after the customer has paid you and only the exact number of copies need to be printed. Profit from the campaign can be ploughed into buying some stock forward to ensure a month or two supply at your fulfilment company warehouse but no huge cost risks. Further sales of copies are then pure profit.

The initial inspiration for using Kickstarter as a pre-order site for a product was gained from having observed and then spoken with Chris Birch, the founder and CEO of Modiphius Entertainment.

He has successfully had funded five Kickstarter Campaigns:

- Achtung! Cthulhu—The WW2 Keeper's & Investigator's Guides

It raised £177,557 from an initial funding goal of £8,000

- Mutant Chronicles 3rd Ed. RPG

It raised £151,072 from an initial funding goal of £11,000

- The Thunderbirds Co-operative Board Game by Matt Leacock

It raised £234,602 from an initial funding goal of £20,000

- Corvus Belli's INFINITY Roleplaying Game

It raised £346,330 from an initial funding goal of £25,000

For this campaign Chris began with approximately 8,000 subscribing members of the Infinity Fan base.

- Conan Roleplaying Game.

It has raised £436,755 from an initial goal of £45,000

Just over £1.34m already raised through using Kickstarter as the sales medium.

We contacted Chris back in December of 2015 and he gave us his blessing for the project and has agreed to handle our worldwide distribution. This means that as well as the 1.4 million purchasers of Elite: Dangerous, this product will be advertised and promoted to over 30,000 subscribers to Modiphius, see their credentials here, and approximately 500,000 email subscribers to DriveThru RPG.

Back Office and Fulfilments

Kickstarter comes with two options for the back office side of things with either Pledge Manager or Backer Kit. Both will manage the pledges, allow for the backers to purchase further items before checkout and then survey each backer at the end of the campaign to give them another opportunity to [buy] extra things unlocked through the stretch goals.

For fulfilment we will be using the same company that Modiphius use unless Frontier wish us to use their recommendation?

Pledge Levels

A full list of the various levels is set out in Annex A

Suppliers

A full list of suppliers and contact details are set out in Annex B

The costs and ongoing financial tracking of purchases will be done in the first instance by either Pledge Manager or Backer Kit. For pre campaign forecasting and profit modelling we have produced a working spreadsheet which contains the cost per unit and profit per unit and per pledge level. Available on request

Stretch Goals

If only 0.5% (approx. 7,000) of the people who have purchased Elite: Dangerous, bought a printed copy of the Core Manual (£30 pledge) we would raise £210,000 on this Kickstarter Campaign. A similar percentage can be used for subscribers to Modiphius and DriveThru RPG.

It is therefore prudent to have a number of stretch goals which can be bought and paid for after the end of the campaign. Unlike the main pledge contents, it is accepted by many that the delivery times on these stretch goals are not immediate but with all the items sold through the campaign we will keep a full schedule of estimated delivery dates on the KS front page.

If we raised significantly more than our stretch goals are currently prepared for then we can create further titles in the range but pay freelance writers to produce this content. We have a number of individuals that Chris Birch from Modiphius can recommend but we would also be happy to take advice and guidance from Frontier.

A sample list of Stretch Goals is set out in Annex C

Production Timescale

The main Core Manual, the 4 supplements and the New Players Guide will be authored by Olive Hulme.

The completion dates (including a month print run and delivery) are:

End of August, 2016	Elite: The Role Playing game—Core Manual
End of September, 2016	Supplement 1—Military Missions
End of October, 2016	Supplement 2—Exploration
End of November, 2016	Supplement 3—Espionage
End of December, 2016	Supplement 4—Super Traders
End of February, 2017	New Players Guide

NB: for all PDF's, subtract a month.

For all other titles the majority of the writing will be subcontracted out to approved RPG freelance writers (unless any Frontier Staff wish to get involved?) and should be available 3–4 months from the completion of the Kickstarter campaign.

Our Team

[Redacted for privacy]

Case Study: Artovision Acquires IP License with Only a Sample

Stuart Sandler started Artovision with his son Jackson when he realized the item he wanted—a shadowbox (a 3D artwork display) of the Atari 2600 videogame *Pitfall*—did not exist. If they wanted one to enjoy, they would have to create it themselves.

It took some time, but Sandler and Son found a method to print directly on acrylic, giving the shadowboxes the look they wanted. With the help of a printing company and a woodworker, they produced prototypes.

Sandler *père* is a font designer by trade, and he earns his living from licensing. He knew that to reach the level of success he wanted, he would have to partner with other IP holders. He also decided to acquire rights *before* he went into production. Sandler says, "We knew we had to start with licensing those properties up front, or else we couldn't have started in the videogame marketplace, which was our primary focus."

He hired a licensing agent, who told him to hop on a plane so they could attend the Las Vegas–based Licensing Expo. There was a catch, of course: because they were essentially attending at the last minute, they couldn't get appointments to speak with IP licensors, which are booked well in advance.

But Artovision managed to get in front of decision makers anyway. As the licensing agent spoke to receptionists, describing the shadowbox as a collectible platform for artwork, Sandler held a sample. It had instant impact, and he secured several five-minute

---

PROFESSIONAL EXPOS AND TRADE SHOWS: THE OTHER CONVENTIONS

Grow your potential market by vending at related industry expos. If you sell horror-themed items, consider HAuNTcon, which serves the Halloween retail community. If you have a line of toys, check out Toy Fair New York. Buyers and licensors attend these expos, so consider attending only after you've reached a level of success and are looking to expand.

meetings at the expo. This led to licenses with Konami, Intellivision, and beverage company Icee. The success of these licenses led to licenses with other companies.

When Artovision is not working with someone else's IP, the two-person company creates art based in the public domain.

Lessons from Artovision's IP Acquisition

When trying to acquire IP using samples of your work, don't use their (or anyone else's) IP. When putting your work in front of IP holders, stick with unique or public domain samples. According to Sandler, "Licensers don't appreciate you coming to them with examples of their IP in your format." In other words, don't approach Marvel with your Spider-Man fly trap. Use a character of your own creation. In other other words, you need to ask permission, not forgiveness.

File a provisional patent, then a patent. After Artovision received enough engagement, Sandler filed a *provisional* patent. Provisional patents cover your work for one year while you're preparing your actual patent. According to the U.S. Patent and Trademark Office (USPTO), a provisional patent "enables immediate commercial promotion of invention with greater security against having the invention stolen" (*www.uspto.gov*). For more details, see "Creating Your Own IP" on page 9.

Hire a licensing agent. Experienced licensing agents know the business and have connections you do not. They will charge a percentage of your earnings—sometimes as much as 50 percent. Reach out to a geektrepreneur with a license and ask for a recommendation or find an agent through an internet search.

Attend an expo for licensees. In pandemic-free years, there are expos around the world where you can get in front of the people who can make your licensing dreams a reality. For example, the Licensing Expo (*www.licensingexpo.com*) provides a matchmaking service for licensors and potential licensees.

Bring your A game. Don't show any item that has a handmade look to it. Your sample has to display a high level of quality.

Be unique. Any company can make an iPhone case. Only you can create something special. Sandler says, "If you want to connect with a license, you have to bring something fresh to the market that [license holders] feel is going to be valuable to their IP."

There are opportunities all around you. Sandler says that when it comes to "small video- and boardgame companies . . . the developer is only an email away." Sandler, as well as Spidermind Games, cautions that small IP holders may not have the bandwidth to respond to your IP queries. Be persistent but respectful.

So What If Your IP Is Infringed?

In a perfect world, your intellectual property is yours. Your fans respect that, and they would never think of earning money from your work without paying you some sort of licensing fee.

You may be shocked—*shocked!*—to know that this isn't always the case. You have the same recourse as large companies do. This is your intellectual property, after all. Just take a deep breath and read on:

 If you find someone infringing, don't automatically assume they're bad people. Never attribute to malice that which can be explained by ignorance. Someone may genuinely not know that a small, below-the-radar work is yours. Inform the infringers.

Consider a licensing deal. If you like their product, consider offering a licensing deal, as well as hiring a lawyer to hammer out the details. As with larger companies, licensing is good for you, because it generates income and works as another source of advertising. Yours is likely a small business, and theirs could be equally tiny. Create a licensing agreement that benefits you both.

Send a cease-and-desist letter. If the infringers don't respond to your request for a licensing deal and continue to produce items based on your IP, then it's time to send that C&D letter. And if they don't respond to that, know you have both ethics and Judge Dredd, um, that is, the law on your side.

THE BUSINESS OF GEEK BUSINESS

You make geeky goods and manage to sell a few items. You do it for love, and you earn a couple of bucks along the way. Perhaps you're a one-person shop, or maybe you have the help of a spouse or friends. You're a small business owner.

If you think that a simple transaction isn't enough to create a business, you'd be surprised. In 2018, i.e., pre-pandemic U.S., according to the "Small Business Profile," there were 30.2 million small businesses, that is, a business with fewer than 500 people earning less than $7.5 million a year (*www.sba.gov*). "Only a third of them had employees." That means there are approximately 20 million small businesses without employees . . . and only 10 million with.

According to the *Guardian* report "The US Census Bureau Says There Are 32m Small Businesses. They're Wrong," these sole proprietorships don't tend to be power earners, as "76.2% of businesses that had no employees accounted for just 4% of sales of all small businesses" (*www.theguardian.com*).

You don't have to earn hundreds of thousands of dollars, or even thousands, to have a business. But you can and should register, to prove that you have a business and not a hobby.

Why Register Your Business?

If you decide you want to go into business for yourself, congratulations. You've done it.

So why would you want to *register* your business when you've done just fine selling without it? After all, you're just making a couple of bucks. In geeky layman's terms, you're farming copper, not gold.

Because there are benefits that go with registration.

You Get to Deduct Expenses

Deducting your expenses saves you money, as it can reduce the amount of tax you need to pay, and you'll owe less money to the Internal Revenue Service (IRS) at the end of the year.

Supplies, repairs, advertising expenses, utilities, contract labor, and more are deductible. Want to sell your goods at conventions? You can deduct the cost of travel, hotel, food, plus expenses related to building inventory.

If you dedicate a space in your home for your business—say, an office or workshop—you'll be able to deduct a part of your rent or mortgage. The key word here is *dedicate*. Your home workshop won't be eligible for deduction if it's used for other purposes, such as storing your Krampus Day decorations.

You can deduct most of your health insurance premiums, even as a sole proprietor. (Speak with your accountant and insurance agent for details.) This is good news if you're doing well enough to quit a job that provides insurance. Or if you've never had insurance to begin with.

You Put Yourself into a Better Mental State

Declaring a business puts you in a business frame of mind. You're not just making geeky crafts. You're working for yourself.

It's Good for You and the Economy

Your view on taxation is your own. But the fact is, the more money you put into Social Security, the more money you take out again later, at age sixty-two or older. Future You nods enthusiastically.

Another way to think about it: *not* declaring income and paying taxes based on that income has its own problems. Like fines and penalties, jail time, or egads, having your passport revoked (see "Didn't Pay Your Taxes? You Could Lose Your Passport" at *http://money.com*).

You Qualify for Small Business Loans and Programs

The U.S. Small Business Administration (SBA) gives out loans during disasters, pandemics included. In some cases, you can qualify for six months' worth of debt relief.

VISIT THE U.S. SMALL BUSINESS ADMINISTRATION

The SBA has small business development centers across the country, where you can learn to build and grow your business. The service is sometimes free, while some SBA centers charge a small fee. Find your nearest SBA branch online.

PROVE YOUR BUSINESS ISN'T A HOBBY

Only businesses can deduct losses from their income. Hobbies cannot. The Internal Revenue Service suggests several ways for you to prove you're running a business and not just trying to snag tax breaks to support your pastime. They include

Actively try to earn money. If you collect celebrity signatures and plan to deduct the cost of acquisition, actively sell them rather than display them at home. You need to offer them at conventions, markets, or on a website.

Change your methods to increase profitability. If your celebrity-signatures website draws minimal traffic, prove you're trying to earn money by perhaps optimizing your website for online searches or even investing in advertising. You can also increase your profitability by selling articles with amusing anecdotes about how you acquired these signatures.

Maintain your records. See "Fun with Bookkeeping" [p. 58.]

Register and run a business. This is where the fun begins, for varying degrees of fun.

A NOTE ABOUT ETHICS

A geeky business is an ethical business. Even if you can't emulate the powers of galactic guardians or star warriors, as a fan, you can emulate their values in your work.

Green Lantern Corps members take an oath to fight evil. Geeky businesses should likewise take an oath to be honest and fair with the community. It's up to us to shape the world into a place we want to live and work in.

Ethical businesses

Treat their employees, customers, and business partners fairly. If you say you're going to pay your contractors, pay them; don't make excuses or point blame. If you say you're going to provide a particular service, provide that service. It's what Superman would do.

Respect others, regardless of their race, sexual or gender identity, religion, or planet of origin. Don't be hatin' on, say, the good people of Latveria, just because Doctor Doom is Latverian.

Comply with the law—and more. Ethical businesses abide by the law, and laws include paying employees, accurately representing your products and services, doing business with companies that have transparent supply chains, and not lifting someone else's IP.

Are honest, even when it hurts, such as when a delivery date slips. A reputation for honesty will often save your relationship with your customers in a crisis—and any comics fan knows there's always a crisis brewing somewhere.

Treat their business rivals with respect. As Obi-Wan Kenobi and Anakin Skywalker know, always have the high ground. Don't badmouth your competition. Compete responsibly.

Even if you prefer to cheer for the supervillains, you still need to keep an eye on ethics: Businesses whose leaders show integrity, responsibility, and compassion are more profitable than businesses with unprincipled leaders (see "Measuring the Return on Character" at *https://hbr.org*), and customers prefer to do business with companies that aren't creepy (see "3 Reasons an Ethical Business Leads to Profits" at *https://onlinemba.wsu.edu*). You also save money by not having to pay for expensive lawsuits and/or henchmen.

Post your code of ethics—kind of like the Ferengi Rules of Acquisition, only nicer—on your website or wherever you do business.

STARTING THE BUSINESS

So how do you actually start your own small business (and unless you have Danny Rand money, your geeky business will likely be a small one)? Let's just say it's a journey of—does the math—a bunch of steps.

GET THE IDEA

Some of you are already making, crafting, sewing, building, designing, drawing, painting, and writing. But if you have only a vague idea of where to put your geeky energy, see the final chapter [p. 185] for ideas.

GET THE MONIES

See "Funding Your Business like a Boss" [p. 99.]

DETERMINE WHAT CATEGORY OF BUSINESS YOU SHOULD CREATE

Without meaning to sound like a broken Voyager record, consult your accountant or tax attorney to see which type of business is best for you. But the three most common options to structure small businesses are

> Sole proprietorship
>
> S corporation
>
> Limited liability company

Consider the pluses and minuses of each (see "Choose a Business Structure" at *www.sba.gov*).

GET A BUSINESS LAWYER ON A BUDGET

Willow Volante saved money creating an S corp by using the help of a local law school. Because these law students were still learning their trade, she did not pay for their services, only filing fees.

Sole proprietorship

Anyone in the U.S. can become a sole proprietor. This business is run by you and you alone. You can hire other people, but the company is yours.

You can start as a sole proprietorship, then level up to another type of business whenever you feel like growing.

Your business assets are your personal assets, and vice versa. Get sued, and you can lose both (hence the reason why many choose other structures).

If you're planning to expand, getting a bank loan can be difficult.

S corp

This entity requires both federal and state registration, so it's twice the initial paperwork.

You can have shareholders, but they must be U.S. citizens.

The owner's profits, and some losses, can be carried by the owner, not the business, reducing corporate tax.

Your business may continue if you leave the company.

You're required to file annually; that includes a filing fee.

LLC

"Limited liability" is an important legal protection. Your personal assets (house, life savings) are safe from lawsuits related to your LLC.

You don't need to have a large company to have an LLC; you can register a "single-member" LLC.

You don't have to pay corporate tax—just personal.

You must contribute to Social Security and Medicare.

Establish a Business Location

Many geeky businesses are home-based ones. Still, check with your local laws before you begin. Although running a variety of businesses from your home is perfectly legal, in some cases, seeing clients there is not legal: while you can ship customers a geeky-themed welcome mat, you might not be able to roll it out for them.

While many budding geektrepreneurs can't take on rent payments, according to the Small Business Association, some businesses qualify for tax incentives if they're located in disadvantaged neighborhoods (see "Pick Your Business Location" at *www.sba.gov*).

Get a Business Name

Your business name reflects your work, as well as acts as an invitation. The work of, say, "Cthonic Creations" will be speaking directly to people who enjoy eldritch horrors while sending a subtle signal to fans of fairy princesses that your work may be too dark for them.

A good business name is short and memorable. A better business name leans into your product, like "Cthonic Creations" would, if you made horror-themed sculptures or face masks. The best name of all has a domain that hasn't been registered by anyone else. [See "Create a Website," p. 83.]

Other tips:

Avoid *Q* and *Z* when you mean to use *K* and *S*, as you'll be frequently misspelled.

Don't use symbols, which are either invisible on web searches or actually change the meaning of a search (for example, a word after a minus sign is deleted).

Consider your own name . . . unless your name is Lois Lane.

Still no ideas? Try an online business name generator.

Register Your Small Business with the Government

When you're ready to register your small business, here's where you visit the website or office of your state's Department of Commerce (or **hire a geeky lawyer**) to guide you through the process. Laws vary, but some states require you to register with the federal government, your state, and your county.

Get a Tax License

Getting a tax license is the point where your business really gets the official officialness. With a tax ID, you can open a business bank account. You can also pay the government and your contractors/employees (if/when you have any) under this ID. Your future employees will thank you.

You can find the link to acquire a tax license online on the "EIN Assistant" page of the IRS website (*https://sa.www4.irs.gov*).

Many states require you to get a state tax license too. For a breakdown on state taxes for small businesses in general, visit Etsy's helpful Seller Handbook on its website.

Get a Business Bank Account

Take your tax license, your business-filing documentation, and your government-issued ID to your bank to create a business account. After you've created

GIVE YOUR BUSINESS NAME ROOM TO GROW

Catherine Elhoffer (Elhoffer Design, clothier) initially focused on making sweaters and cardigans. But the name Elhoffer Knitwear would be a limitation now that she designs dresses too.

your account, place all of your business-related earnings here. When you make a business-related payment—for example, acid-free bags for your comic book sales—it should come from this account.

Always keep your personal and business funds separate. Don't (seriously, don't) cross the streams and use your business funds to pay for personal expenses. Your accountant will thank you.

REGISTER YOUR INTELLECTUAL PROPERTY, IF ANY

[See "Creating Your Own IP," page 9.]

ACQUIRE BUSINESSES LICENSES

Businesses that require federal licensing—commercial fisheries, mining and drilling operations—are unlikely to be geeky ones. But you may need a *state* license if you plan on running, say, a geek-centered tattoo parlor or a business that makes customized vampire teeth. Check with your state's Department of Licensing to be sure.

CONSIDER BUSINESS INSURANCE

The Small Business Administration recommends you insure your business (see "Get Business Insurance" at *www.sba.gov*). Insurance is yet another expense that some may not be able to afford at first, but coverage offers peace of mind (and also . . . coverage) against those random acts of the gods. Look into either home-based business insurance or a business owner's policy. Expect your insurance prices to increase the moment you hire employees.

FUN WITH BOOKKEEPING

Keeping your financial accounts is important, says professional bookkeeper (and part-time chainmail jewelry maker) Katie DiGiacinto. "Keeping track of your [incoming and outgoing] expenses teaches you what your business does."

Find organizing your finances tedious and stressful? DiGiacinto recommends looking at it another way: "You're working on a puzzle. What you're spending and what you're selling are the pieces." Bookkeeping is just putting a puzzle together. And as you know, geeks are really good at puzzles.

RANDOM NOTES ON REGULATIONS

★ Let's say you have a machine shop for creating cosplay armor. It turns out that machine shops have regulations set by the Occupational Safety and Health Administration (OSHA). Keep your business compliant—and protect your workers and yourself—by following OSHA regulations.

★ It is illegal in the U.S. to sell nonprescription contact lenses—no matter how often you see them at conventions (see "'Colored' and Decorative Contact Lenses: A Prescription Is a Must" at *www.fda.gov*).

★ You need a cosmetology license if you want to style hair. But you don't need a license to style a cosplay wig.

KEEP TRACK OF YOUR EXPENSES

As soon as you open your business door, anything that touches your business can be tracked and written off. "If any receipt has a dollar sign," says DiGiacinto, automatically keep it and file it by date.

Your lunch with a client who wants a personalized geeky cake topper is a business expense and can be deducted for a tax break. If you're driving to the post office, where you're mailing your Etsy creation, you should track your mileage; while you're at it, keep the receipts for your gas too. If you don't hold onto them, you can't take deductions. Therefore, you pay more taxes.

Take advantage of this perfectly legal way to reduce your tax bill. Sometimes it results in a refund, which puts money in your bag of holding.

KEEP TRACK OF YOUR TIME

Track the time spent on work-related processes. Whip out your cell phone and time how long it takes to design that escape room or paint that miniature. Tracking your time helps you price your work more accurately. [See "Pricing Your Items," p. 61.]

DiGiacinto says that when she works chainmail in a new way, she sometimes charges for her learning time. "Sometimes I charge, and sometimes I don't. But I get to choose."

KEEP TRACK OF YOUR ASSETS

An asset is any permanent/semipermanent item with financial value that you need to run your business. For example, if you're a maker of geeky dresses, your sewing machine is an asset, while your pins and fabric are not; your laptop is an asset, while the coffee you need to fuel it is not.

Assets lose value over time (also known as "depreciation"); for example, a computer you purchased for $1,000 is worth only $800 next year. Consequently, you can get a tax break as your assets age, which is why it's important to track them—depreciation is the tax break that keeps on giving.

Oh, and although software is intangible, nonphysical property, it can be depreciated if you use it to run your business (for example, CAD software for your 3D printer).

USE BOOKKEEPING SOFTWARE

Use software like QuickBooks, Xero, Sage, or even Excel to track your expenses. Accounting software can reduce inevitable human error; plus it helps you or your accountant prepare your taxes faster than they would with paper. Which saves you money.

Need help organizing your expenses?

Hire a geeky bookkeeper.

HIRING HELP

Don't spend days struggling to build a website when you're as tech-savvy as Captain America. If a necessary piece of your business can be done better, faster, and at a reasonable price by someone else, give it to the professional.

If your business is doing exceptionally well, you might want to hire an employee to be the Beaker to your Bunsen. That takes managerial skills, so take a class on management or ask managers you admire for the secrets to their success. Then find the right people and train them. Tell your hires what you expect, step back, and let them do their job.

PRICING YOUR ITEMS

You've produced your geeky charm bracelets, and you're ready to get charming. But how much do you sell them for?

Many artists undervalue their work and are afraid to price items accordingly. To them, David Pea has the following advice.

Add Up Your Expenses

"You have to . . . make enough money to make it worth your while to sell [the items]," says Pea. He recommends:

 Take the price of your materials.

Consider the time it takes for you to make your product.

Add some of the cost to run your business (for example, electricity, a storage space, free samples for press, etc.).

Factor in the price of shipping.

Voilà, you have a base price.

"Numbers don't lie," says Pea. "We don't inflate things to price ourselves out of the market. When we have products that sell at $2,600, you can bet that our costs are higher than two grand."

Don't Forget Markup

Markup doesn't exist simply to earn a profit. It helps provide a financial cushion. For example, Pea buys fabric in bulk. So if he has an order for ten gloves and needs only four yards of material, he still has to make a minimum purchase order, say, one hundred yards.

"The reality is," Pea says, "these markups serve to keep the business running."

Ask Your Customers or Friends

Pea has developed relationships with customers who can be objective, "Whenever a product is ready, I'll have images and data, and I pick up the phone and say, 'Here's what we're making. As a fan, what would you pay for it?' Nine times out of ten, their feedback is really close to what we're projecting to go to market with."

Before you acquire long-time customers, ask your friends. If they aren't willing to spend $1,500 on a handmade white gold necklace, you might want to purchase a less-pricey metal to work with instead.

CHECK THE COMPETITION

If you make something simple to produce, like a T-shirt, go to the sites of your friends and friendly competition. If they charge $30 for a shirt and $45 for a hoodie, whereas you charge $60 for a shirt and $75 for a hoodie, they may have more customers than you.

Is your price higher because you use finer materials? With hand stitching? That makes yours a higher-end item. Use that description in your marketing. [See "Marketing 101," p. 71.]

A GUIDE TO THE GEEKY NONPROFIT

The Organization for Transformative Works. Extra Life. Games for Change. These aren't businesses. They're nonprofit organizations, each dedicated to causes near and dear to the geek heart. They also happen to be 501(c)(3)s, a type of nonprofit that gives tax breaks to those who donate. If your superhero persona would rather help the helpless, instead of fighting evil, this may be the vocation for you.

CREATE YOUR OWN NONPROFIT

Nonprofits are organizations on a mission. Meeples for Peeples, for example, distributes board games to children's hospitals and low-income families; among other activities, Geek Partnership Society sends children ages ten to fourteen to space camp.

Running a nonprofit is also as much work as, if not more than, running a business:

 Nonprofits have more accounting rules than businesses.

Every dollar raised needs to go toward your mission. You have to justify *all* of your expenses to your donors.

If you say you provide legal aid to comic book creators and you don't, the IRS will revoke status as fast as you can say "Shazam."

You're required to file articles of incorporation (complete with filing fees), report income, declare your board members' salaries, hold annual shareholder meetings, take minutes, grow your assets, and more.

Your nonprofit can't be used for personal gain or to further someone's political career.

On the upside:

Most of the money you spend on your nonprofit is exempt from both state and federal taxes.

Whenever someone gives to your cause, their donation benefits them in the form of tax breaks.

You and your board of directors may draw a salary.

Captain America thinks *you're* a hero.

GET HELP WITH YOUR NONPROFIT

The Foundation Center (FC)—itself a nonprofit—offers free classes on fundraising. It also has a database of 140,000 funders, along with notes on which causes they fund, so you can find a foundation or big-ticket donor whose values are aligned with your nonprofit. Although you have to pay monthly to use this database online, you can use it for free at FC's offices in New York City, Cleveland, San Francisco, Atlanta, and Washington, DC.

Write a Short Mission Statement

A mission statement spells out the purpose of your nonprofit. For example, "The Comic Book Legal Defense Fund is a nonprofit organization dedicated to protecting the First Amendment rights of the comics medium," and "The Organization for Transformative Works is a nonprofit organization, established by fans in 2007, to serve the interests of fans by providing access to and preserving the history of fanworks and fan culture in its myriad forms."

Recruit Your Board of Directors

Gather a superheroic team of like-minded individuals who support your mission, typically a minimum of three members. Laws vary from state to state.

Get Your Papers in Order

 File articles of incorporation with your state—and don't forget those filing fees,* so budget accordingly. (You can find samples online.)

Get your *state* tax ID number (not your federal tax ID. That comes later).

Apply to reserve your nonprofit's name with the IRS. (As with a business, search online first to see if the name is already taken.)

*Good news: You can accept donations even before your nonprofit is officially registered, so you don't have to pay your registration fees out of pocket. But you must have your paperwork processed within twenty-seven months.

When you receive your 501(c)(3) status, your donors can then apply for an amendment of their taxes for the year they contributed to your worthy cause.

Hold Your First Board Meeting

Develop your operating plan and your by-laws. For example, some by-laws set term limits, which means that the board members may change, but the mission remains the same (just like the rotating roster of X-Men). Also, determine who can open the bank account and who has access to it. Remember to take notes, i.e., minutes, at each and every board meeting. You can find samples of minutes online.

Oh Look, More Paperwork

 File a Form 1023, which gets you your 501(c)(3) tax-exempt status. (Smaller nonprofits that expect to raise less than $250,000 a year can file a Form 1023-EZ.)

Get your *national* nonprofit tax ID number at *www.IRS.gov*.

File for state and local tax exemptions. Each state has different forms. Visit the National Association of State Charity Officials (*www.nasconet. org*) to locate your state's website.

Open That Bank Account

When you head to the bank, don't forget to bring your paperwork.

Start Fundraising

Besides actually fulfilling your mission, fundraising is now your job. Get to work.

In 2018, foundations, individuals, corporations, and bequests donated $427 billion to help do-gooders do good (*https://givingusa.org*). However, acquiring those funds isn't easy money; you'll be competing with 1.5 million nonprofits in the U.S. alone.

Send Receipts

Mail or email receipts to everyone who has donated. If you're a 501(c)(3), donors will need a receipt for their taxes. Don't forget to add a few kind words of appreciation.

File Your Tax Forms Annually

You will file an IRS Form 990 during tax time. Your nonprofit may be exempt from federal taxes, but you'll still have to report the details of income and expenses.

Challenges of a Nonprofit

Keeping your nonprofit afloat is every bit as challenging and time-consuming as growing your own business. But your mission—such as improving literacy through comic books or teaching children how to create their own videogames—can be even more rewarding. Here are some challenges you'll face.

Paperwork Is Work

Don't fill out your forms yourself. Both Melinda Johnson of Meeples for Peeples and David Vetrovec of the Geek Partnership Society filled out their forms incorrectly. In the case of Johnson, she lost two months of time while reapplying. In the case of Vetrovec, he temporarily lost his group's nonprofit status. "It was humbling ... standing in front of the board, explaining that *I* was the reason for losing our status." (He reacquired it soon after.)

Avoid this situation by spending the money—you can anticipate $5,000 or more—to have a lawyer handle your paperwork for you.

Nonprofits Have to Show Fiscal Responsibility

A nonprofit has to invest whatever money it has to benefit its mission. When the IRS saw on the Form 990 that the Geek Partnership Society had thousands of dollars in a bank account, the government reached out to ask Vetrovec, "Why aren't you investing it?"

Vetrovec explained why the nonprofit's money needed to remain liquid rather than be placed in a six-month CD: so the nonprofit could attend a convention. The IRS accepted the explanation. "You have to remember this is not your money you're dealing with," Vetrovec says.

Raising Money Is Hard

Money does not magically flow to your coffers because you have started at a nonprofit. No one at the Geek Partnership Society nor Meeples for Peeples draws a salary, and they rely solely on donations and auctions at conventions to fund their mission. If you would like to draw a salary one day, you should consider hiring a grant writer (**hire a geeky grant writer**).

It's Easy to Flub That "Don't Use Your Nonprofit for Personal Gain" Clause

Vetrovec says that the Geek Partnership Society was unable to sell its T-shirts through a shirt designer's site because that could be considered benefiting the shirt designer. How did the nonprofit know? It found a lawyer who consults on minor questions for $50.

You Need to Be Completely Transparent About Your Income

Not only do you need to post your financial statements (i.e., a Form 990) to your website, but also anyone who draws a salary has to post their earnings too. Visit the Comic Book Legal Defense Fund's website (*http://cbldf.org*) and peruse their financial data for a detailed look at a nonprofit's earnings and expenditures.

You Need to Be Careful Where You Fundraise

If you plan on fundraising outside your state, that new state may require you to register with it as well. Many nonprofits work around this restriction by placing a Donate button on their websites, so donations come to them directly.

UNUSUAL BENEFIT OF BEING A NONPROFIT

Running a nonprofit has one real benefit for its board: nonprofits convey an amount of respectability. Sometimes being a charity can confer a positive cachet for businesses that you work with.

When the landlord tried to raise the rent at the office that the Geek Partnership Society leases, the nonprofit said outright it couldn't afford the higher fee. But the landlord and the nonprofit found a mutually beneficial arrangement because, Vetrovec opines, the landlord wanted a nonprofit in the building.

"Businesses will respect you if you do a good job," Vetrovec says. In this case, this respect translated to a break on rent.

SELLING YOUR WORK AND SELLING YOURSELF

Some geektrepreneurs limit their sales to an Etsy shop or perhaps a small circle of friends. But the successful ones—the ones who have turned their geeky hobby into reliable sales—recognize that creating merchandise is only part of the job. The rest involves selling it.

Although some of you are effortless self-promoters, some of you don't care to draw attention to yourselves. That's okay. Geektrepreneurs have an active, vocal fandom to help you sell your wares.

In this chapter, you learn how to sell your work . . . and sell yourself too.

MARKETING 101

Selling a product is more than making something amazing, putting it up on Etsy, and waiting. If you want people to tell you, "Shut up and take my credits," you need a marketing plan. Here's how you begin.

INTRODUCTION? LET YOUR WORK DO THE TALKING FOR YOU

Are you shy? Find the idea of being snapped by Thanos preferable to engaging with customers, even geeky ones? You're not alone.

When you speak to scary strangers or energy-sucking sociovores, consider it as educating the customer. How can they buy your fabulous geeky item if they don't know about it? If you need emotional distance between yourself and other people, focus on the value of your cool creation, not on yourself. Also, a good salesperson knows how to listen to customers, to understand what they want, so that they can better provide it to them. And listening is a skill in which introverts excel over their extroverted fellow business owners.

BRANDING

Identify your brand. Your brand is the voice of your business. It's what you say, how you say it, and to whom.

David Erwin, former executive creative director of Warner Bros. and DC Comics, says, "You have to understand what your brand represents. What do you want that brand to create in the mind of that person who's purchasing?"

Because you and your customers are geeky by default, your message has to be fine-grained. Do you produce high-end goods for geeks with thick wallets? Does your product have a soupçon of the risqué to it? When building your brand, consider the most important elements of your business you want to convey.

You can instantly understand your brand by answering the following questions: What does your favorite fandom mean to you? For example, if the object of your geek attachment is Harley Quinn, what is it about her that you find appealing?

As a class clown, Harley attracts playful pranksters in *DC Super Hero Girls*. She speaks to survivors of abuse in *The New 52* when we see that she's washed that Joker right out of her red-and-blue hair. She's still chaotic yet loyal and resourceful as a partner to Poison Ivy in the animated adult series *Harley Quinn*.

Simply answer which of these Harleys you prefer ("chaotic" and "happy"; "strong" and "resilient"; "fun-loving" and "loving"). Now that you know what you love, take these qualities and target an audience with them. That's your brand.

A GREAT EXAMPLE OF BRANDING IN FANDOM

It's called whiskey

Although the final season of Marvel's *Jessica Jones* aired in 2019, its Twitter feed is still a great illustration of branding. Check out Marvel's PR team's posts (*https://twitter.com*), filled with cutting comments in her voice, like, "It's not me, it's you. It's definitely you."

Jessica's brand is "sarcastic" and "embittered." Because of this, you will never see a twee, floral Jessica Jones throw pillow. But you may see a mug or martini glass with one of her more popular quotes: "It's called whiskey."

Notice that these descriptive words have an emotional component. You want a brand that inspires a positive emotional reaction, no matter how small the brand. It can make your work memorable.

Erwin says, "Once you understand the position of your brand and the identity of the brand, then you have to start communicating that through your products. You need to be consistent in your ongoing messaging with the consumer. Consistency is everything."

Distill your business to its basic values, and there you have your brand.

Case Study: Tea & Absinthe: Steampunks Sell Tea . . . and the Idea of Tea

When Pacita Prasarn and Daniel Myers first decided to sell at conventions, they weren't sure what they wanted to sell. They sat down and decided what aspect of the fandom they wanted to represent: steampunk—a popular movement dedicated to alternative, science-forward, mid-to-late Victorian-era aesthetics, which has its own dedicated conventions.

From there, Prasarn and Myers asked themselves, "How did people in the 'steampunk era' enjoy themselves? There was tea and there was absinthe." With that, a geeky business was born. They created Tea & Absinthe, a line of geeky teas and absinthe barware.

Tea & Absinthe's brand is made clear at every convention the company attends:

 Charming: A steampunk-themed booth in the middle of a 21st-century convention makes passersby smile.

Sociable: The staff is sociable, a reminder of the fact that tea is imbibed with friends.

Soothing: When people drink tea, they're taking a moment to recharge and calm themselves.

Even as Prasarn and Myers branched out from steampunk cons to media conventions, their consistent use of branding continued to inform their business, from the logo to their convention booth. "A lot of people use wire [for the backdrops of their booths]. We wanted wood," which suits the retrofuture aesthetic. They could have sold tea from plastic boxes. Instead, they use metal ones, which are more on brand for their business, with their logo pasted on each tin. In addition to tea and barware, Prasarn and Myers sell teapots and infusers, as well as cups and books that could be found in the home of a proper steampunk enthusiast.

Prasarn and Myers' clothing also reflects this aesthetic, and the couple, along with their assistants, wear steampunk finery and/or cosplay at each convention.

Many of the items in their booth look as if they came from a tea shop, circa 1890. This look was carefully designed by Prasarn, an experienced retailer, and Tea & Absinthe's booth is an oasis of calm compared to other more eye-arresting displays.

Prasarn and Myers recognize they're not just selling tea. They're selling what tea represents.

SOCIAL MEDIA

Comic book, board game, and toy stores aside, most geeky businesses exist online, rather than brick and mortar. Therefore, your digital presence is how you interact with much of your customer base. And your words, images, and videos can easily be seen by millions of actual and potential customers, thanks to social media.

Social media has been a transformative tool for sales and customer outreach, allowing small and large businesses to reach their customers with a few keystrokes. As Jordan Dené Ellis of Jordandené (clothing and accessories, *jordandene.com*) says, "I don't think we would sell anything without social media."

A 2020 survey on social media by Hootsuite reports the following statistics for monthly visitors (as reported in "140+ Social Media Statistics That Matter to Marketers in 2021" at *https://blog.hootsuite.com*):

 Facebook: 2.5 billion

YouTube: 2 billion

Instagram: 1 billion

Pinterest: 335 million

Statistics for daily visitors:

Snapchat: 218 million

Twitter: 152 million

Additionally, if you search Discord, you will find over 100,000 sci-fi and related channels (see "Tags Similar to Sci-fi" at *disboard.org*).

With that many people vying for each other's attention, it's hard to make your signal rise above the noise of the internet. You could read books (of which there are many) about social media sites (of which there are many), and still, you wouldn't know all there is to know about social media. There are, however, general lessons that geektrepreneurs have learned over the years that you can benefit from. Better yet, they apply to all social media platforms.

Post

When it comes to acquiring followers, Jamie Broadnax of Black Girl Nerds (online magazine, *https://blackgirlnerds.com*) says, "There's no magic trick. Just spend time on the platform consistently." Broadnax, who focuses her attention on Twitter, says, "You can easily get lots of followers just by engaging: tweeting, retweeting, quote-tweeting."

Pacita Prasarn posts mostly on Facebook. Prasarn sees a direct correlation between social media and sales, particularly updates. "When I post that a product is back in stock, sales come in." That's the power of social media: being able to communicate your message to countless readers at the same time.

Post Some More

Post as much as possible, to keep yourself in the public eye. While some businesses manage one social media post a week, others post every day, some even three times a day. How much you post is up to you, but the more you post, the more you engage with your audience.

Don't have the time? When you find a few spare minutes, you can schedule your social media posts in advance. Services for scheduled posts include Hootsuite, Tweetdeck, SmarterQueue, Post Planner, Later, Buffer, and others.

NOT EVERYONE WANTS TO USE SOCIAL MEDIA

As one interviewee said, "There's only so much time in the day. If I can be creating, that feels like a better use of my time than shouting into the ether." This interviewee may be more comfortable with this decision than other business owners because their arresting artwork is better seen in person, at conventions, than online.

If you're not comfortable with social media, consider outsourcing it. [See "Hiring Help," p. 61.]

WHIP OUT THOSE HASHTAGS AND MENTIONS

Let's say you sell prestyled cosplay wigs. When you're posting an image of a cosplay wig you've styled to look like Gamora from *Guardians of the Galaxy*, make sure to use hashtags. Include *#Gamora* and *#GuardiansoftheGalaxy* on your posts. Social media users looking for a Gamora fix can find you with a simple hashtag search.

When you post your premade cosplay wigs, consider @-tagging the actor who played the character (in this case, Zoe Saldana). One day, you may be followed by that star and their star power. Broadnax says that the social media account of Black Girl Nerds grew "when celebrities followed us. That brought in a lot of followers."

Make sure you're tagging the right account. Fans of George R.R. Martin on Twitter have mistakenly followed @GRRM when the author's real account is @GRRMSpeaking.

Don't Just Post Your Business: Post Your Brand

Prasarn posts pictures of the two Tea & Absinthe owners at conventions or working in their storage space, humanizing the business and reminding the audience that theirs is not a large, faceless company but a small mom-and-pop shop that appreciates your patronage. Prasarn also posts tea-related facts and humor. Broadnax of Black Girl Nerds likewise posts more than links to articles or pictures of media events: the site and its social media accounts cover the politics of being Black in America. Both sites remain on brand.

Stay on Target

Broadnax says that when she started using Twitter, "I used to see what was trending and jump into the conversation." Although it may have received attention, and therefore followers, the site has steered away from that. "I used to talk about everything, things not even related to the blog, and I think that messed up our brand identity."

However, Broadnax says that she follows geeky Twitter trends, so if, say, Harley Quinn is trending, she will give it a mention.

Post About Geek Culture in General

Your brand, above all, is geeky. Remind your potential customers that you feel the pain of missing geeky gatherings during a pandemic, just like they do. Share your (spoiler-free) thoughts on your favorite shows, your epic videogame kill streak, the book you couldn't put down. These posts start a conversation.

Build Relationships

"When we post something new, I look at feedback, I look at the comments, and I respond to messages. It's how we get to know people," says Ellis. "Our customer relationships are mostly on social media. It really is a huge part of our entire business model. Most of the people who come see me in person at events and stop by the booth are people who I've met online first."

Be kind, interesting, and entertaining on social media, and show your potential customers you're the type of person whose business they want to patronize.

Ask Customers to Post About You

Ask for pictures of and from fans, and get permission to share them. Ellis says, "We ask for our customers to post photos, and they get a special gift if they do. We end up seeing our biggest fans because they post photos [of themselves]. And we get to know them."

Retweet when fans speak well of your work. Positive reinforcement is the gift that keeps giving. And don't be afraid to ask someone to post your work. (The worst they can say is, "No, you suck." But at least you know where you stand.)

JOIN ALL SOCIAL MEDIA SITES TO BLOCK POTENTIAL CYBERSQUATTERS

Even if you plan to concentrate on only one social media site, you should still join the other popular ones. This way, you can make it harder for others to take your business name.

Don't Forget Smaller Social Media Sites

Geeky business owners have name-checked Tumblr, Imgur, Reddit, and DeviantArt as places where they've received commissions or made sales as a result of posting their work. You may not have similar luck, but you'll never know unless you try.

KEEP YOUR BUSINESS AND
PERSONAL ACCOUNTS SEPARATE

If you're posting personal opinions to your business account, readers aren't able to determine who they're listening to. If your business produces geeky cosmetics and nail art, you may put off fans when you post about your other obsessive hobby, juggling geese.

Keep your personal life on a personal account. And not just about politics and religion: as Prasarn says, "No one cares that I'm menstruating."

Case Study: Fannish Business Owner Uses Social Media to Break into Her Own Fandom

Miriam "Max" Salzman, the owner of Etsy shop Summer of String, combined their talent for making friendship bracelets with their fannish passion for the BBC series *Orphan Black*. Their social media outreach was so successful that their bracelets appeared on their favorite series. Salzman even earned their own IP license—proof that while fans have always celebrated their passions, now companies are celebrating their fans.

Let's rewind.

Salzman was moved to create *Orphan Black* string bracelets when they fell hard for the 2013–17 show about a wayward young woman who learns she's one of many (many!) clones. Salzman tried to find merchandise and came up empty. "There was nothing," neither on Etsy nor the rest of the internet, they said. If they wanted to wear *Orphan Black* anything, they would have to make it themself.

Salzman already had a talent: making string bracelets, which they had learned in summer camp. So they married their talent with their passion and created *Orphan Black*—themed designs.

Meanwhile, in an effort to meet other *Orphan Black* fans, they created a Tumblr account and invited people to play an *Orphan Black* Cards Against Humanity game. Although they hadn't deliberately set out to promote their work, in the course of conversation with twenty other players, they would occasionally mention their new bracelets and ask *Orphan Black* friends to repost their work. Their bracelets sold slowly but surely.

Later, one of the producers of *Orphan Black*, Mackenzie Donaldson, posted to Twitter that she was looking for *Orphan Black*–based fan art to highlight on her show's podcast. Salzman sent her some bracelets—not only for her but also for the rest of the writer's room. (Salzman works as a stage manager, so they wanted to reward the people who worked behind the scenes.)

The staff liked the gift so much that they immediately thought of Salzman when a storyline required a bracelet. When *Orphan Black*'s production company Boat Rocker Media reached out to Salzman, they offered them a licensing deal. Salzman still retains the licensing deal to produce *Orphan Black*–related string bracelets, which they sell on Etsy.

Although Salzman has never earned enough money through Summer of String to support themselves, thanks to their fandom, they met their best friends and roommates, and they have seen their work appear on screen. Making and selling string bracelets might not be a wild financial success, but by every other metric, Salzman is wonderfully accomplished.

As a takeaway for the geektrepreneur, Salzman created opportunity by sharing their work with fans who wanted to see it.

REMIND READERS ABOUT YOUR BUSINESS

Broadnax made a splash on Twitter when she live-tweeted shows from her point of view as a nerdy woman of color. The downside: the Black Girl Nerds Twitter page became so popular that people didn't think to visit her website. Black Girl Nerds hired a social media manager to promote the site, which is home to articles, reviews, and the BGN store.

SHARE OTHER PEOPLE'S IDEAS—
EVEN POST YOUR COMPETITORS

If you're a blogger, shout out an interesting article on another blog. If you're a T-shirt designer, name-check another small business. They may do the same for you. A rising tide lifts all boats.

According to research conducted in 2018 by CoSchedule, the best times to post business-to-consumer messages are as follows (in Eastern or Central time) (https://coschedule.com):

Facebook
- 9–10 a.m.
- Noon–1 p.m.
- 4–5 p.m.

Instagram
- 8 a.m.
- 1 p.m.
- 9 p.m.

Twitter
- 8–10 a.m.
- Noon
- 7–9 p.m.

LinkedIn
- Noon

Pinterest
- 8–11 p.m.
- 2–4 a.m. (Because there's no sleep in Pinterest?!)

TIME YOUR POSTS

The best days to post:
Facebook
- Thursday–Sunday

Instagram
- Friday

Twitter
- Saturday–Sunday

LinkedIn
- Wednesday

When you're growing your audience, don't forget people outside of your time zone or even country. Repost important tweets so people on the West Coast, the UK, and Australia, for example, can see them.

CREATE A WEBSITE

While social media is an excellent tool for reaching customers, it's limited to a few characters and images. It's also ephemeral, and your important posts continually make way for new ones. Websites, however, provide an anchor to your information. A website is your knowledge base, the repository of information pertaining to your business. [See "What to Put on Your Website," p. 85.]

Jordan Dené Ellis says that websites are useful because, "You can curate a shopping experience for your customers and show what's important and different from other companies."

Most importantly, a website is your digital storefront. With an online shopping cart, you can sell your goods in a few simple clicks.

Websites are not free, however. You will need to spend money on your domain name. They also can be frustrating for those who don't know their way around the innards of a content management system (the back end of a website, an area that only you see). However, you don't need much time or skill to build a website, and there are dozens of instructional sites and YouTube videos to help you on your way. (Or you can **hire a geeky web developer**.)

In addition, you can earn money (albeit, a small amount) from your website each time someone clicks on it, thanks to ads served by online advertising services like AdSense. [See "Advertising," p. 94.]

USE MARKETPLACES. BUT DON'T RELY ON THEM

Online marketplaces like Etsy, TeeFury, Threadless, Zazzle, Redbubble, and more are frequented by millions of potential customers. But you shouldn't rely solely on a third party to run your business; you're constrained by their interfaces, and their terms of service can change without notification—possibly to the deficit of the seller (you). Join multiple marketplaces, so if you don't like the new terms of service of one site, you have others to help generate income.

ACQUIRE A DOMAIN NAME AND PLACE TO HOST YOUR SITE

Start by purchasing your domain name through registration sites like Joker, NameCheap, Domain.com, or others. Remember to place a note on your calendar to renew your domain name, so it can't be snatched up by someone else.

After you purchase your domain name, you need to find a place to host your site. When considering an online provider, consider how much help you need and where you get support. Your teenage relative may be technically savvy yet unreliable during exam time. Consider hiring a professional if you're in danger of extended downtime.

Build it yourself. Skill level: Emperor. At a mere $5/month, you can have virtual cloud hosting from services like Linode, Digital Ocean, and Vultr. The work is yours, all yours.

Get a managed virtual host. Skill level: Darth Vader. Managed virtual hosts like Cloudways provide 24/7 technical support, mirroring, and staging. It's still a lot of work.

Hire a website designer. Skill level: Padawan who knows they're ready for the Trials. A website designer can create a customized look that works for your business, and you can **hire a geeky designer** who understands your customer base. You need to run the back end.

Use a website builder. Skill level: Gonk droid. Website builders such as Weebly, Wix, and Squarespace charge a monthly fee for a customizable website. There's also IndieMade and Big Cartel, if you want a website designed for artists. These require almost no technical skill.

KNOW HOW YOUR SITE WORKS

Think of running a website like driving a car: you don't need to be a mechanic to drive, but you should know the basics of maintenance. Likewise, you don't need to know how your backups work, but you should know which buttons to press in order to restore from a backup. Make sure you know enough so that you're not dependent on a developer for every simple task. If you work with a developer, ask questions and take notes of the answers. And while you're at it, make sure you create automatic backups of your site. Future You will thank you.

WHAT TO PUT ON YOUR WEBSITE

Now that you have a website, you should let potential customers know who you are and what you sell. Include the following:

Your logo. A good logo is simple, clean, recognizable at a distance, and unique *enough* (as an example, many major corporations use their business name in Helvetica). Also, consider your competition. If you want to start your own animation company, avoid any asset that, say, resembles the Pixar lamp.

Your goods and services. Your best work should shine. Post pictures of your work (and if you don't have them, **hire a geeky photographer**), as well as pics of your items being enjoyed by your customers. Do you do customized work? Insert your clever creation here.

HIRE A GEEKY MODEL

If your work requires models, particularly when it comes to geeky fashion, hire fans. Your fan base will recognize themselves in your work, and your models will make good cheerleaders for your business. Remember that fans come in all shapes, races, genders, and ages.

Product categories. Do you make axes *and* two-handed swords? Separate them into categories. If you work with multiple fandoms, you might want to have sections for "TV/Movies," "anime," "comics," etc. Don't forget a category of your best-selling items.

A shopping cart. Fans will appreciate it if you accept PayPal, Venmo, and all major credit cards. In addition, add a checkbox as customers are checking out so that they can subscribe to your mailing list. [See "Build a Mailing List," p. 89.]

Your FAQ. Answer your frequently asked questions here. They include your international shipping policies, allowability of returns or exchanges, and length of turnaround time. If, say, a pandemic is harshing your turn-around time longer than usual, address any problems and negative comments quickly and professionally on your front page.

Contact information. Use a form that requires a user's name and email address in addition to their comments. This provides you with a small layer of privacy over merely placing your email address on your site.

An *"About You" section.* In a few brief paragraphs, tell your and your company's origin story.

Your press. Share any press about your work on social media here. Include a link to the article too, so the original publisher can get that extra click, and as Missandei said on *Game of Thrones*, "All shall prosper."

Links to your social media and Patreon. Although many potential customers will come to your site via social media, the reverse may also be true. Make your social media links prominent—especially your Patreon (p. 117), if you have one.

A convention calendar. Let your customers know where you'll be in advance, barring pandemics and/or alien invasions.

Also Seen on Geektrepreneur Websites

Catherine Elhoffer's Elhoffer Design website flashes the names of customers and the purchase they made on her website, through an app called FOMO. It's a great way to connect your business to a larger fandom. It also provides the appearance of success, even if your goods are selling less like hotcakes and more like lukewarm cakes.

Danielle Reichman of LittlePetal (convertible dresses, *www.littlepetal.net*) filmed several tutorials of her convertible dresses, so customers could learn how to create multiple styles with the same dress. In addition, she honored her customers in a series of short interviews, "Badass Babe of the Week."

Jordan Dené Ellis's website The Sartorial Geek (*http://sartorialgeek.com*) holds geeky fashion challenges and offers prizes to the winners. She also posts the submitted pictures on her website.

Volante Designs offers experience points ("XP") for every purchase and every social media post that customers make. Every 100 XP earns $1 off on their next purchase.

Extend Your Reach with These Marketing Tips

Here are some other ways to get your product's name in the minds of fans without resorting to planting an *Inception*-like message in their dreams:

Start a Facebook group. Reichman has her own Facebook group, the Little Petal Alliance. Members of the group are encouraged to post their news and random thoughts, as long as they're supportive of each other.

Create a music playlist. Ink & Lyre (role-playing game content provider) created Spotify and Apple playlists to enrich their customers' role-playing experience. It's a fun and inexpensive tip.

Use labels. Selling clothes? Add a label to your garments so that your customers know who it is they're wearing. Online stores like WunderLabel and DutchLabelShop make clothing labels so you don't have to.

Reward fans with small discounts. Because 10 percent off is the thought that counts. Include a coupon with your sales items, to encourage repeat business. In addition, Jordan Dené Ellis offers a discount to fans who sign up for her mailing list.

Create a Newsletter

The purpose of a newsletter is to drive traffic to your site while building a relationship with your audience. If you're hesitant to put in the work that a newsletter takes, consider this: Jordan Dené Ellis says that most of her sales correspond with the release of her weekly newsletter.

Your newsletter should not be lengthy. Don't kill yourself trying to write engaging but ultimately disposable text month after month. It needs to convey only two or three simple ideas as well as links to your website and your products. If you have more to say to your customers, say it on your blog, but link to it in the newsletter.

Topics to cover in your newsletter can include

- A convention memory and how it ties in with your products

- An amusing work-related anecdote

- A fact you learned about your particular industry

- Customer reviews

- The inspiration for your most recent craft

- A look at the gorgeous materials in your upcoming production run

- Interviews with customers or fellow geektrepreneurs

Ellis also recommends offering discounts in your newsletter and perhaps exclusive items to reward your current customers.

Newsletters don't require much writing talent. But before you send out your newsletter, make sure a second pair of eyes gives your copy the once-over (**or hire a geeky proofreader**) to catch any errors that may have wormed their way in.

Build a Mailing List

Companies like MailChimp, Zoho, Sendpulse, and MailerLite will help you create a mailing list—and in some cases, track how your newsletter performs—for little or no money. But first, you need to populate it with the addresses of your current and potential customers. Here's how to acquire them:

Collect email addresses at conventions. (See "Conventions: Ways to Contact You" p. 144.)

Ask your friends. Friends almost by definition share your interests. Many of them would like to be included in your mailing list, if only to see what you're up to as a geektrepreneur.

Ask your friends to share with their friends. Ask your buddies if they would like to help you grow your business by inviting *their* friends to your list.

(Don't take it personally if they don't. Some people avoid anything that looks like promotion, while others are naturally shy.)

Mention your mailing list on your website and social media. It's logical: No one can sign up for your list if they don't know about your list.

Make sure your customers have a way to opt out of your mailing list. Be ye warned. It's a violation of the CAN-SPAM act to enroll customers in a mailing list without offering them a way to opt out.

If you have the budget for it, throw a raffle. Offer a modest prize to anyone who subscribes to your mailing list. To keep things fair to the second power (fair and squared), the prize should also include current subscribers.

When to Send Out a Newsletter

Keep your business on your potential customers' minds by sending out a newsletter once every two weeks. But if you don't have the bandwidth, there are still opportune times to reach out to readers:

When you're announcing and/or offering a new product. Give your customers first dibs on your newest product, to thank them for their patronage.

When you have something to say. Are your vendors late with their shipment, thus making you late with yours? Keep the clients informed in the newsletter—and remind them of what it is they're anticipating.

When you have something to celebrate. Did you sell out of a print run of your limited edition artwork? Had your favorite artist praise you on Twitter? Spread the word to people who are invested in you and your work.

SAMPLE NEWSLETTER

As fans of [Your Business Name] Cookie Cutters know, cutters aren't just for cookies: you can use them to cut pie crusts, to make your pies look as good as they taste.

Fan [Insert fan's name here] sent us this lovely image of her super-heroic pie, which she created using our superhero cookie cutters [link to superhero cookie cutters]. Thanks to this, she helped her son [insert name] celebrate his tenth birthday in style. She was kind enough to share her recipe too. (And a happy belated birthday to you, kid!)

[Insert pic of decorated cake]

Recipe:

[Insert fan-provided recipe]

A LOOK AT OUR PRODUCTION

We had our cookie cutters 3D-printed right here in our hometown of Gotham City by Lucy Fox Studios, courtesy of 3D artist and engineer and owner, Lucy Fox.

[Insert pic of Lucy Fox]

Lucy purchased an industrial 3D printer back in 2018 and taught herself the use of CAD software. Her work includes printing finials and scrollwork for an architectural firm. So what did she think of the cookie cutters? "It wasn't my most complex job. But with the cookies that I made to test the cutters, it was certainly my most delicious."

Next time you see her in town, thank her for her mad skills with the printer. For all your 3D printing needs, hire Lucy [her business URL].

HERE'S WHAT PEOPLE ARE SAYING ABOUT OUR COOKIE CUTTERS

[add a hyperlink to your website on the words "cookie cutters"]

[insert images of cookie cutters]

"I loved the cookies I made with your fantasy cookie cutters—
and so did my kids."

—Klimt Barton

"Used your horror cookie cutters. Clean-up wasn't a horror. Thanks."

—Bruce Bannerman, MD

"Thanks for the cookie cutters. They arrived on time and
in good condition. Also, what's not to love about cookies?"

—Natasha TimesNewRomanoff

SPECIAL SOCIAL MEDIA OFFER

If you use our fabulous cutters and tag us on Instagram, Twitter, or Facebook with @[*YourBusinessName*]CookieCutters, we'll give you 10% off on our next production run. Cookie cutters make a great gift, and as we know Winter Is Coming (and that means winter holidays).

· ·

Still uncertain as to how to write a newsletter? Sign up for the newsletters of fellow geektrepreneurs and learn from their experience. You can ask them for some pointers too. Or **hire a geeky writer.**

SEND OUT A PRESS RELEASE

Press releases are five or six paragraphs' worth of information designed to pique the interest of editors and writers. If you catch their attention, they may turn your press release into an article. This converts their readership into your potential customers.

You can find multiple samples of press releases online. As you'll see, you don't need to be eloquent. All you need to do is write (1) what it is you're announcing, (2) why it's interesting, and (3) when and how it's available.

Make sure you include images of your product, preferably from a professional photographer Also, if possible and practical, offer to mail samples of your work to writers and editors, so they may review your product.

Send out your press release to geeky markets. Don't forget local newspapers too. And if you make, say, geeky cookie cutters, consider nongeeky food magazines and blogs.

KNOW YOURSELF. AND YOUR CUSTOMERS

The U.S. Census Bureau recommends conducting a survey of your clientele (*www.census.gov*). Potential questions include your customers' age range, gender, state, fandoms, and where they purchased your items.

The results may surprise you. You may think your customers are college-aged, female *Supernatural* fans, but you may learn that you're selling mainly to male thirtysomething Bronies. With this information, you can adjust your merchandise list accordingly.

More importantly, this survey will give you statistics that advertisers want to see, to determine if your audience aligns with their potential market. [See "Advertising: Websites and Podcasts," p. 125.]

To encourage participation, you may want to offer your customers a small discount on their next purchase or offer a raffle prize.

It's better to know more about your customer than less, because geeks know that knowledge is power.

ADVERTISING

Geeky businesses have spent up to 25 percent of their gross income on advertising. Here's where geektrepreneurs have spent their advertising dollars:

SOCIAL MEDIA

Facebook, Instagram (owned by Facebook), and Twitter allow you to spend as little (or as much) as you'd like to promote your business. You can even tailor your ads, so one ad will be seen by as many people as possible while another targets, say, gamers.

These social media sites don't actually "sell" ad space. Instead, they auction it off. Set a budget (say, $5.00/day) and your ad will compete with every other ad in the same type of business, that is, the same vertical. If other artists are trying to sell their ads for $0.59 each, and you bid $1.00, your ad will be displayed, not theirs. Once your spending limit is met, your ad campaign ends.

Social media sites also allow you to "boost" or "quick promote" a post, putting that particular post more prominently in people's feeds. When Quentin Weir (*www.elderwoodacademy.com*) sees one of his Facebook posts is successful, he spends money to boost it. "This allows us to get that post out to more than just our own audience," says Weir.

Conversely, Joel Meadows (*www.tripwiremagazine.co.uk*) says that he posts general articles with the intention of boosting them in advance. "Sometimes it increases our traffic to that particular post, sometimes it doesn't." But this has increased his overall readership, he says, "at least in the short term."

Social news aggregate site Reddit also uses a pay-per-click model.

POPULAR WEBSITES

Sites that actively seek advertising dollars post their demographics. If your customer base aligns, you might want to shunt your advertising budget there.

While some sites require a hefty minimum buy (for example, Fark requires $5,000 or more), other sites charge less (Tor.com charges $1,500 for one week); the more trafficked the site is, the higher the advertising ask. These amounts are out of reach for a starting business, so don't pull out the wallet too early; you can get attention from social media posts and a mailing list.

SEARCH ENGINE ADS

You can advertise on search sites such as Google, DuckDuckGo, and Bing using keywords (search terms that you specify in advance). When people search on keywords related to your business—say, "modern gothic romance"—your ad will be promoted to eager readers.

As with social media, on search engines, there are no minimum spends, and your advertising campaign lasts as long as your budget does.

PODCASTS

Podcasts generated $708.1 million in advertising in 2019 and were expected to earn $1 billion in 2020, according to the *U.S. Podcast Advertising Revenue Study* (*www.iab.com*). What this means for the geektrepreneur who wants to buy ad space: the podcasting industry is ready, willing, and able to take your money. So, sponsor an episode of your favorite geeky podcasts.

MICRO-INFLUENCING

Influencers are media socialites followed on their platform of choice (particularly Instagram) by hundreds of thousands of people, and for a fee, they will showcase your products. Micro-influencers are the same, only with fewer followers.

In the geekosphere, micro-influencers can have an even smaller audience, in some cases only one thousand followers. However, their posts tend to be finely grained—for example, one may post mainly about LGBTQ+ comic books, and another, collectible card games—and their audience can be highly engaged with the subject matter. Yours too, if there's an overlap.

Micro-influencing worked for Daniel Hodges, co-owner of Ink & Lyre (Dungeons & Dragons content provider, *www.inkandlyre.com*). Hodges sponsored an episode of *Web DM* (Dungeons & Dragons vlog, *www.youtube.com*) [see below]; for a fee, *WebDM* mentioned Hodges's work.

The result, Hodges says, "changed my entire marketing strategy." After earning back "ten or fifteen times more" than what he paid," Hodges says, "we still get people who trickle in from that one video we sponsored. . . . Micro-influencers are so much more valuable [to my business] than Facebook ads."

The biggest problem Ink & Lyre has had with influencers? Hodges reached out to several people he considered good candidates . . . and only *Web DM* responded to his query.

So how do you acquire your very own micro-influencer?

Reach out to someone you're personally influenced by. Ask them if they'd be willing to to let you sponsor them.

See which of your social media followers has a large following. If they post about their love of Clark Kent, and you sell Clark Kent-inspired spectacles, introduce yourself.

Search on appropriate hashtags; then see who wrote the most popular posts. Again, browse their timelines. If they post about subjects in your realm of geektrepreneurship, offer to pay them, so they can point their followers at you.

Ask fellow geektrepreneurs for recommendations. They can tell you which influencer worked best for their business.

Hire a geeky PR person. If you have woolongs to spare, they can locate micro-influencers for you.

For more insight into what micro-influencers do, or to start your own geeky micro-influencing business, head over to chapter 9, "Geek-Centered Work," [p. 185].

SELLING YOUR WORK AND SELLING YOURSELF VIA COLLABORATION

You sell a fabulous product. Someone you know sells a similar fabulous product. Consider combining the power of both of your fandoms to create something new . . . and expand both of your fandoms at the same time. Collaborate.

Daniel Hodges of Ink & Lyre says that collaborations have been an important part of growing his business. Here's his take.

Case Study: Dungeons & Dragons Business Shows How Collaborations Can Work for Everyone Involved

Hodges wanted a way for RPG gamers to "engage with our content," that is, spells, dungeons, races, and subclasses that he writes and his wife/co-owner Lauren designs. After spending time on Instagram, he decided, "One of the best ways to do that is shared hashtags."

One December, his wife created the hashtag *#25DaysofDND* and invited Instagrammers to join them in their social media adventure. They created daily prompts as jumping-off points for creativity.

Hodges reached out to the D&D Coalition, a platform for role-playing content providers. He says, "We sponsor[ed] a magic item on their account during our collaboration. And then *they* collaborated with other creators and had them join in our *#25DaysofDND* hashtag as well." Fans soon joined in, sharing the artwork inspired by the prompts.

The results were as good as encountering a Level 13 owlbear when you're a Level 18 Druid whose favored enemy happens to be an owlbear.

"We saw a lot of Instagram account growth from that, because [the D&D Coalition is] absolutely right within our target market," Hodges says. "The people who follow them are also the same people who would follow us. . . . From an engagement standpoint, it certainly helped us a lot."

And now, says Hodges, "Sometimes when we have a very specific item that [The D&D Coalition] love, they add to their shop." The D&D Coalition then pays Ink & Lyre a commission when someone purchases that item.

Even after *#25DaysofDND* ended, the fans who showed up continued to follow Ink & Lyre.

TIPS FOR SHAMELESS SELF-PROMOTION

Are you extroverted and have no shame? These tips will certainly get you attention.

Go to a fabric design site like Spoonflower.com and create prints based on your own IP (say, a comic book). Make clothing from that fabric, and wear it in style.

Create a QR code of your website or preferred social media site. Use it as your cell phone's wallpaper, so you can quickly show it to interested fans.

Sign up for Help a Reporter Out. HARO is a website that pairs journalists with experts in their field, and as someone who owns your own growing business, you are an expert at what you do. Respond to appropriate queries. If a reporter quotes you, congratulations. You've just received free publicity.

The same is true for sites like Podcast Guests, which pair potential interviewees with podcasters.

Have a catchphrase from your YouTube channel or a character you've created? Print it on a T-shirt and sell it.

Tweet or post as a character you've created, especially if your character has a very specific point of view.

Just plain ask people to follow you on social media.

FUNDING YOUR BUSINESS LIKE A BOSS

Starting a business takes a solid idea, endless energy . . . and funding. As the saying goes, "It takes money to make money," and as the geekier saying goes, "No bucks, no Buck Rogers."

So how do you acquire the Republic Credits you need to turn your dream into reality? Seventy-five to 80 percent of small businesses are funded by the owner, according to the "Small Business Statistics" page of the Chamber of Commerce. As for the rest, "16% of businesses are funded by bank loans, while loans from family and friends account for 2–6% of initial small business funding" (*www.chamberofcommerce.org*).

Start your business free and clear of debt by funding it yourself. But you don't have to pay for all of your start-up costs from your own pocket. Crowdfunding has become a way for some business owners to earn money, even before they begin.

Here's a look at how to fund your business.

THE FIRE MOVEMENT

Suggestions for funding your business would not be complete without a mention of the FIRE movement—that is, Financial Independence, Retire Early. This movement promotes frugal living in exchange for freedom from [*insert your day job here*]. Proponents recommend cutting nonessential spending, then investing your money in a way that provides a 4 percent yield.

You can find information about FIRE on websites such as Mr. Money Mustache (*www.mrmoneymustache.com*) and in books such as *Your Money or Your Life* by Vicki Robin.

FIRE isn't for most people. But the ones who successfully FIRE quit the jobs they don't love so they can pursue the work that they do.

BEFORE YOU BEGIN

You're about to embark upon a financial adventure, where the "adventure" means "risk" and "financial" means "your money." Before you accept this quest, minimize that risk with a plan.

CREATE A BUDGET . . .

Some of you can build your initial inventory based on material you already have at home (looking at *you*, sewers with piles of unused fabric). But others will need to spend gold pieces on equipment, tools, or a workshop space.

Ask yourself what you need to start your geeky business—for example, potential podcasters might want a better-than-average microphone—write down your list of expenses, and start saving.

AND STICK TO IT

You've set aside money to create bespoke boardgame pieces for best-selling games. You've planned on spending $500 for a quality 3D printer. But you've identified a better printer for $600, only $100 more. What do you do?

A. Take away from another part of your budget, say, hotel expenses, to make up the $100 shortfall,

B. Run up that credit card, or

C. Earn an extra $100 before you buy the printer.

You already know the answer.

Many a geektrepreneur has indeed run up their credit cards in pursuit of their goals, and while spending an extra $100 on a printer won't cause financial ruin, this extra spending adds up. Recognize that if your business isn't a financial success, you'll still need to pay off that debt. And you know what happened to Han Solo when he owed Jabba money. . . .

SAVE MORE THAN YOU'D THINK

Reece Robbins, co-owner of Frontline Gaming (store and more, *www.frontline-gaming.org*), says that although he and his partners bootstrapped their gaming store for $10,000, it took the effort of two years of nonstop work to see something like success [see "Case Study: Frontline Gaming Extends Its Reach with YouTube," p. 124].

Robbins says, "In a perfect world, you'd have a year's worth of operating costs in reserve capital, because it gives you time to learn from your mistakes."

JOIN A MAKERSPACE AND SAVE MONEY

Don't buy expensive equipment until you've earned enough money to pay for it. Instead, join a local makerspace. Makerspaces are shared spaces that provide equipment for a monthly fee. Depending on the location, a makerspace can have a phenomenal array of equipment, from power tools, soldering irons, CNC routers, 3D printers, and sewing machines. Larger makerspaces even hold classes.

Prices vary, depending on the location and type of equipment you have access to. Because you share equipment with everyone in the space, you may have to wait to get your hands on the tools you need. But you can prototype your idea to see if it's viable before you drop mad stacks on the business.

How to Fund Your Business

Let's look at ways geektrepreneurs have funded their successful geek businesses.

THE DOS AND DON'TS OF FUNDING YOUR BUSINESS

Never invest anything you're not prepared to lose. If you look to raise money from friends and family, make sure they don't invest anything they're not prepared to lose.

Don't get a bank loan to start your geeky business. A bank loan should be used to grow your business, not start one from scratch. Your bank will expect a fully fledged business plan and your credit score, so start building it up now.

Don't touch your retirement savings. Unless you've cleared it with your financial advisor, don't touch this money, not even for the geeky business of your dreams. If you don't have a financial advisor, get one so that they too can tell you not to touch your retirement savings.

Don't max out your credit cards. They may save you if you suffer an unexpected crisis, so treat them as a last resort.

Keep Your Day Job(s)

A traditional job provides a steady paycheck and schedule. Because you can't guarantee you'll see a return in your new job, a job will help replenish the income that outgoes. Unless you have a spouse with a good job that pays health insurance; have retired with Social Security, a pension, and/or stocks; are heir to a family fortune; or have a well-funded business partner who pays expenses while you do the physical labor, keep your job until you know when it's the right time to leave.

Get a Part-Time Job

A part-time job can provide a sense of structure *and* much-needed cash. Bonus points if your part-time job is dull, which allows you to spend your creative energy on your own work. Besides part-time work, there's also gig work; side hustles include Instacart, Lyft, TaskRabbit, and more.

Spend as Little Money Possible

You may want to buy everything you need to create a full-fledged business, but unless you can spin straw into gold, don't give in to the urge.

Look for fire sales, garage sales, flea markets, and auctions. Ask your friends and their friends if they can spare any equipment you need.

Buy the best you can afford, not top-of-the-line. You can level up your gear when the orders come in.

Upcycle whenever you can. Etsy artists purchase low-cost thrift-store paintings, then paint geeky characters into the picture; their costs could be lower than if they had purchased brand-new canvases and frames.

Learn to repair equipment so you can renovate used machinery or to get more life out of the equipment you already have. YouTube videos can teach you how.

Fund Over Time

Some projects require more money than you have on hand. You can still progress your business, albeit slowly. It took four years for Spidermind Games to produce its first board game [see "Case Study: Spidermind Writes a Successful IP Proposal," p. 28]; to create a documentary based on his fandom, it took Troy Foreman . . . longer than that.

Case Study: Troy Foreman Makes an Award-Winning Documentary Based on His Fandom

Forget *The X-Files*. Troy Foreman believes that Chris Carter's *other* series, the slow-burning horror *Millennium* (1996–99) starring Lance Henriksen, was his apex accomplishment. One day, Foreman discovered a site called Back to Frank Black, whose goal was to revive the show. He joined the campaign and, along with fellow fan James McLean, created a podcast called *Millennium Group Sessions*, which ran from 2007 to 2010.

In addition to episode reviews, "Mainly what [MGS] was known for was interviewing cast and crew members." To secure the interviews, Foreman joined IMDB Pro and contacted the agents of actors who appeared, explaining the MGS focus. "Over the podcast's life span," Foreman says, "we pretty much interviewed everyone from the show."

"There are people out there who let their fandom get the best of them, because they're starstruck. You need to approach the people that you want to interview in a professional manner. If you're attempting to turn your fan experience into something professional, you have to be professional," says Foreman.

Foreman's friends kept the *Millennium* fire alive with a book called *Back to Frank Black*, to which he contributed. (All proceeds from the book went to star Henriksen's favorite charity, Children of the Night.) Eventually, Foreman wrapped up his fan campaign with "one final big project, a documentary, as a thank-you to Chris Carter and the people who created the series," he says.

As McLean had other commitments, Foreman found another business partner, Jason D. Morris, maker of the fan film *Millennium Apocalypse*. Together, they created *Millennium After the Millennium* in 2019. The film took two years to complete, but it drew on work that began twelve years prior. Because Foreman had interviewed the cast and crew for his podcast beginning in 2007, because of his work on the *Back to Frank Black* book—and remember, the proceeds were donated to Henriksen's favorite cause—and because of Morris's films, they were able to secure all the on-camera interviews they needed.

Millennium After the Millennium eventually won two Best Documentary awards and received six other honorable mentions. As a bonus, when Foreman spoke to Chris Carter about the documentary, he jokingly asked for a part in the final season of *The X-Files*. Carter hired him as an extra for the final episode of Season 11.

Foreman and Morris are working on their next projects . . . which will hopefully take less time to complete.

BUILD AN INEXPENSIVE BUSINESS

A fan who creates and sells crochet, cross-stitch, or knitting patterns of their favorite horror characters has access to several free online programs. Someone with a large science fiction book collection who wants to sell their lesser-read fare already has their inventory. These businesses may not earn much, but they don't cost much to start either.

GO SMALL(ER)

Do you have grand plans to start your own comic book publishing company? Great. Publish a single title first, learn from your first mistakes, prove your successes, then gradually add on more titles when you can afford it.

REDUCE YOUR EXPENSES

A three-bedroom house in central Missouri costs less than a studio apartment in San Francisco. Reducing expenses by moving to a less expensive state or even neighborhood can give your business a boost by helping you trim your living expenses. If your new place has room for you to work, you can write off part of your rent or mortgage on your taxes. [See "You Get to Deduct Expenses," p. 50.]

AND THEN THERE'S CROWDFUNDING

Read on.

CROWDFUNDING

Crowdfunding sites like Kickstarter, IndieGogo, WeFunder, and Patreon are portals that connect makers with potential backers and future customers—and they do it extremely well. According to reports of crowdfunding statistics on Fundly. com, the crowdfunding industry raised $34 billion between in 2001 and 2015 (*https://blog.fundly.com*).

Games in particular have fared very well on Kickstarter, and by 2020, gaming (both video and boardgaming) raised $1.28 billion (see the "Stats" page of *www.kickstarter.com*).

Geeky crowdfunding accomplishments include

The board game *Exploding Kittens*: $8.8 million

Critical Role: The Legend of Vox Machina Animated Special: $11.4 million

Another board game, *Kingdom Death Monster 1.5*: $12.4 million

Fan films, books, comic books—they would never have been produced were it not for the self-interest of strangers, as fans know that backing a project gets them first crack at the item or experience being funded. This means they can possess a craveable object weeks or even months ahead of the direwolf pack.

Exclusive rewards—such as artwork or personalized shout-outs—sweeten the already sweet experience.

TAKE ADVICE WHEREVER YOU FIND IT

YouTube's Creator Academy (*https://creatoracademy.youtube.com*) has advice on how to market your YouTube channel, and some of that advice is agnostic—that is, it works for your business no matter what the platform. The same goes for Patreon (*https://blog.patreon.com*), Kickstarter (*www.kickstarter.com*), and other crowdfunding platforms. Mix and match advice and find the strategies that work best for you.

WHY DO YOU NOT WANT TO CROWDFUND?

At the time of writing, Kickstarter reports over 186,000 successful campaigns . . . and over 495,000 unsuccessful ones, a success rate of 38 percent (see the "Stats" page of *www.kickstarter.com*). Also, 11 percent of campaigns received zero pledges. That's a whole lot of nothing for a whole lot of work.

Crowdfunding also takes months of social media prep work before the campaign has begun. [See "Build Your Network in Advance," p. 109.] That's on top of creating your masterpiece and getting it out the door.

WHY DO YOU WANT TO CROWDFUND?

The most important reason to crowdfund is that crowdfunding campaigns help you raise money from your audience directly. This approach can save you months, if not years, earning the money yourself. Also, every person who backs you wants to see you succeed. Their support is an ego boost that money *can* buy.

CROWDFUNDING ADVICE FROM KICKSTARTER

Oriana Leckert, senior outreach lead for Publishing, Comics, and Journalism at Kickstarter, says, "In the early days of crowdfunding, sometimes just the fact of having a Kickstarter would get you tons of notice. That is not the case anymore. You don't just upload your video, put in some copy, and then magic internet money falls in your lap. You have to take your campaign seriously." She has advice to help you do so.

THE MOST IMPORTANT KICKSTARTER STATISTIC

Leckert says, "The success rate [of Kickstarters] is something like 32 percent, which is low and kind of scary. . . . But if you only look at campaigns that have at least twenty-five backers, the chance of success jumps to around 80 percent," says Leckert.

"What that means is if you're getting just beyond your mom and your best friend, if you have a community that's a little bit bigger than those in your inner circle, if you're doing a little bit of marketing, your chances of success are extremely high," she says.

Build Your Network in Advance

Before you crowdfund, you first need a crowd. Leckert says, "If you are just starting out as a comic book artist . . . you want to work on building your network of support.

"You can gain admirers of your work by sharing it on platforms like Instagram or Hiveworks, increase your subscribers by starting a newsletter on Substack or TinyLetter, and increase your fanbase by making a profile on a site like Patreon."

Create a Promotional Plan

Create your promotional plan, which Leckert says "is all the things that you need to do to assemble your crowd." Answer her questions, and consider the answers your to-do list:

- Who are you going to email?

- What are you going to say?

- How often are you going to email them?

- How will you spend your approximately thirty days [that a campaign runs]? You can't just say, 'Have you given me money today?' every day for a month.

- Can you get press write-ups?

- Can you appear on a podcast?

- Can you find amplifiers who can take your message into your community?

- Who can amplify your message into adjacent communities?

Read, Read, Read

Kickstarter's help section has enough information to construct its own library planet (*https://help.kickstarter.com*). "Kickstarter has tons and tons of resources online, an endless array of videos, articles, and listicles," says Leckert. "There are also category-specific resource pages."

Know When to Start Your Campaign

"It's good to have done some amount of work on the product, something you can demonstrate. It's going to be really helpful when you present your work for money," says Leckert. If you begin your campaign before you have any assets, you may discourage people who need to see more than a proof of concept.

Mail Your Potential Backers Directly

A mailing list is the best use of your time, according to Leckert. "Direct emails have the highest conversion on Kickstarter into backers, by far." [For more on mailing lists, see "Build a Mailing List," p. 89.]

Tell a Story

"Every Kickstarter campaign is a story," says Leckert. "So you have to think about the story you're telling and how to make it compelling to your audience." Here's your opportunity to explain the origins of your project, how it fills a need, and how it will benefit your audience/user.

Get Out in the Real World

"Go to Comic Cons and industry events," Leckert says.

Greater Than Games noted that its board games would not have met its crowdfunding goals were it not for the GenCon and PAX East (*greaterthan games.com*). There, Greater Than Games engaged fans and pointed them toward its Kickstarter.

Be a Gracious Member of Your Community

Leckert says, "Find other [creators in your space] and share your work. Be generous. Don't only ask for support and feedback. Also give it. Be a warm community member and people will be eager to support you as you are to them." Create the rising tide that lifts all boats.

Find Your Online Community

Your friends and future colleagues are out there for you to find. "There's a huge comics community on Twitter. There are myriad Facebook groups," says Leckert. "If you write outer space romance, find other science fiction and fantasy writers, and share your work." While you're at it, share theirs as well.

Use the Right Kind of Social Media

"Go where you're the strongest [on social media]" says Leckert. "If you've never been on TikTok, we don't recommend you start a TikTok just to promote your campaign." If you and your friends naturally congregate on Twitter, stick to Twitter.

Leckert notes, "Facebook is still the social platform that leads to the most backings on Kickstarter, but that is shifting. For example, in journalism, Twitter drives far more backings, because journalists live on Twitter."

Work on Your Elevator Pitch

You need to fine-tune your elevator pitch—that is, a description of your work that can be told in the span of an elevator ride. Frame your business goal to a few attention-grabbing moments, so you can pique the interest of anyone who will listen, online and off. For example, "I'm writing a book full of advice on how geeks can run a business doing what they love."

CROWDFUNDING TIPS—FROM SCIENCE!

Dr. Mike S. Schäfer, professor of Science Communication at the University of Zürich, coauthored the academic paper "Selling Science 2.0: What Scientific Projects Receive Crowdfunding Online?" for the journal *Public Understanding of Science* (www.ncbi.nlm.nih.gov). Schäfer has additional advice for crowdfunders:

- *Use humor.* Schäfer says that humor "makes campaigners relatable and sympathetic, I assume. People do like others who have a sense of humor."

- *Keep your overall funding target low.* The lower the funding target of your project, the greater the chance you'll be funded.

Schäfer notes, "Potential donors give more if they have the sense that the entire project will be successful—so people have the impression of contributing to something real, of really making a difference with their donation. This feeling of efficacy is important and seemingly helps to acquire donations."

Leckert says, "Make sure that you know how to talk about your creative work. It's astonishing how many people forget how to be clear and concise when they're talking about something that's so close to their heart."

Don't forget to practice your pitch on your more judgmental friends.

USE VISUAL ASSETS IN YOUR CAMPAIGN

"Kickstarter is a visual medium, just like the rest of the internet. Be visually appealing," says Leckert. But what if your campaign has no visual elements, say a novel or a radio drama? "Share your book cover. Perhaps you can pay whoever's illustrating your cover for a few more illustrations to put into your campaign. There could be art in the public domain that is thematically aligned with the kind of work that you're doing. Have textual elements that are designed to please the eye," Leckert says.

CREATE A VIDEO FOR YOUR CAMPAIGN

"We recommend having a video," Leckert says. "You don't have to create a visual masterpiece. It can certainly be a direct address from you on your computer or your phone. You want to be inviting, inclusive, excited, and upbeat."

It also helps if you describe how your item will benefit your backers and how you'll spend the funds you've raised. Also include a clear call to action.

If you aren't inclined to make your own video, increase your budget and **hire a geeky videographer**.

ADVERTISING: TO PAY OR NOT TO PAY?

Leckert says, "When you're talking about huge six-figure campaigns, paid advertising can work. But within Kickstarter, we recommend building your own network. You're much better off focusing on sort of organic efforts and community building, as opposed to just trying to pay for [your campaign]," says Leckert.

While advertising works, self-promotion works just as well.

THANK EVERY BACKER

Anyone who backs even a single dollar needs to be sincerely and publicly thanked, even if it's simply a shout-out on social media or your project's website.

MORE ADVICE FOR YOUR CROWDFUNDING CAMPAIGN

ADVERTISE THE LAUNCH

Quentin Weir of Elderwood Academy (role-playing game dice boxes and towers, *www.elderwoodacademy.com*) says when Elderwood Academy launched its Kickstarter campaign, "We spent a couple thousand dollars to promote a post about the Kickstarter, to drive awareness of it."

STUDY OTHER CROWDFUNDING CAMPAIGNS

Look at campaigns that are similar to yours, both successful and unsuccessful ones, and learn from them. What kind of language did they use to entice their potential backers? How many images do they display? How many videos?

Fund some projects that are similar to yours as well, and see how their creators engage with their backers. Also, ask geektrepreneurs with successful crowdfunding campaigns to share their hard-earned wisdom.

DON'T FORGET THE COST OF SHIPPING

While some of you have work that can slide into a manila envelope, and others have items that can be emailed, you may have to consider special packaging, especially if the product is fragile. Make sure you've added the cost to the price of your item. Kindly remind your Kickstarter backers that there will be an additional shipping fee for any items shipped internationally.

DON'T LOWBALL YOURSELF

Jon Lunn says that while some may recommend that you place your Kickstarted item at the lowest possible price point, he cautions against it. "The difficulty with that is, if you just get over that price point, you do end up running the very real risk of overpromising and not being able to deliver without losing money," he says.

Backer Rewards

Backer rewards are extras that motivate those who back modestly into contributing even larger sums. Some rewards are enticing enough to be objects of desire in their own right, such as autographed copies of an item or Zoom chats with the artists. Make sure to limit the number of rewards you offer, however, to give you more time to focus on your project.

Find Simple-to-Produce Backer Rewards

Thanks to print-on-demand companies like Tee Fury, Zazzle, PrintAura, CafePress, PureButtons, and others, you can customize items—for example, T-shirts, refrigerator magnets, coasters, buttons, carry bags, even jigsaw puzzles—to use as Kickstarter rewards. Some companies require a minimum order, say, one hundred units or more; others will offer high-volume discounts. These backer rewards are simple to produce, but they are still obligations that add to the time, money, and effort to deliver your item.

Simplify Your Backer Rewards Even More

Writer Alexandra Erin (*https://twitter.com*) cautions against campaign rewards. "People back you because they like you already. If you're asking for funding for your music and you promise a personalized side story, you've just made more work for yourself."

Simplify your backer rewards by folding them into the work you're already doing. For example, if you're an artist, draw a backer into the background of a scene you've planned.

Also consider these minimal-effort rewards to encourage funders:

Offer a rough draft of your creative work and an explanation of why you went in a different direction.

Provide customized wallpaper of your logo for backers' phones or computers.

Wear a backer's shirt at a photoshoot or event.

Follow your backers on Twitter; retweet ten tweets of your choosing. (For example, you shouldn't retweet their antisocial language or opinions that Iron Man is the greatest Avenger when he clearly is not.)

Create a list of inspirations, such as must-read books.

Invite backers to an online chat with the creators involved in your project.

CROWDFUNDING TIPS FROM INDIEGOGO

In 2016, IndieGogo analyzed 29,000 technology campaigns (see "Technology Crowdfunding Stats: 8 Insights from 29,000 Campaigns" at *https://web.archive.org*). Although these observations are limited to tech, consider the insights gained for a nontech campaign:

Start off with a thirty-day campaign; then extend it to sixty days. Thirty days creates a sense of urgency, while extending the campaign to sixty increases the amount of time you have to raise money.

Update multiple times during your campaign (four updates and beyond). More communication is better than less.

Offer early-bird discounts.

Offer limited quantities.

Add perks during the campaign's run. Backers prefer affordable perks in the $10 to $30 range.

If You've Been Funded

Keep your backers regularly informed of your progress, using your mailing list and social media. Not only does this keep the positive buzz going, but your customers will be more understanding if you have to communicate any delays or problems.

Or . . . If Your Campaign Fails

Many crowdfunding projects don't meet their goal. You can learn from your experience, retool your approach, and try again. Perhaps you can try an altogether different approach. Even a failed campaign results in you gathering a list of potential customers. If you fund your project a different way, you've already built an interested audience.

Patreon

Patreon is a crowdfunding site that doesn't fund projects; it funds the creators of these projects directly. For as little as $1/month, generous fans can help you achieve your creative goals.

According to Patreon, in November 2019, creators in total earned $1 billion from four million patrons (*https://blog.patreon.com*). But not everyone is seeing green. In 2019, only 3.2 percent of patrons earned $1,000 a month or more, as reported in "The Business of Patreon" (*https://techcrunch.com*). Still, the few who are successful on Patreon are extremely successful, with some earning tens of thousands of dollars, and in a few cases, over a hundred thousand per month. (For more Patreon Creators Statistics, check out *https://graphtreon.com*.)

As with crowdfunding, people don't hand you money without expecting something in return. They want to see you create, and they want a piece of the output (examples of patron benefits include exclusive content, content in advance of a general audience, hangouts with you and other patrons, T-shirts or other gifts).

Patreon will charge you 5 percent, 8 percent, or 12 percent per transaction, depending on the level of service you choose. Each transaction also incurs an extra processing fee.

HOW TO BEST LEVERAGE PATREON

Alexandra Erin (*www.alexandraerin.com*) is a full-time author who supports herself with her writing work. Even before Patreon existed, Erin used PayPal as a way for fans to support her work; ultimately, Patreon streamlined her ability to fundraise and communicate with fans. With the exception of selling a few articles, all of her earnings come from the internet, with the bulk of it from Patreon. She gets it by asking for it. Here's how.

Get Yourself into the Mindset That You're a Professional

"Separate what you're doing when you're asking for money in exchange for your work from the idea of 'charity,'" said Erin. "What you're doing is a market transaction, where people who see value in what you are doing are giving you value back."

Erin's father works in financial services. She says, he "doesn't think about 'leveraging a client base,' because for him, it's a mutually beneficial arrangement. Neither side should take advantage of the other. If everything goes well, both sides are coming out ahead, and that's what has informed how I do things," Erin says.

Build an Audience

Erin initially posted her stories on LiveJournal for free. She says, "[Everyone says] 'Don't work for exposure,' and I agree with that. But my caveat is don't work for anybody else for exposure. Do it for yourself." Because she wants as many people as possible looking at her writing, most of Erin's stories are free to read.

Later, Erin decided she needed a social media following in order to get eyes on her work, and she chose Twitter as her public platform.

Straight-up Ask for Money

When writing on Twitter, "Every once in a while, I would throw a PayPal link at the end of a thread, as a tip jar. Sometimes these threads would go kinda viral, and I would get some money from it," she says.

Erin says, "Self-promotion is hard and awkward, even after you've been doing it for years. So I have a little twitter bot that tweets variations on phrases, like 'Hello there! To help support my work, the best way is by joining me on Patreon (*www.patreon.com*). Thank you for reading.' Sometimes it links to my Patreon, sometimes it links to my PayPal tip jar."

Don't Say No to Money

Erin didn't come up with the idea for a PayPal tip jar on her own. Several readers who enjoyed her work suggested it. "I felt no, [my work] was not ready." She soon changed her mind.

"I see people who are much further along [in their careers] and have a bigger following, who are making the same kind of demurrals, 'It's not ready, it's not worth it.'" To them, Erin has the following advice: "Don't say no to money."

Nowadays, when someone asks Erin to put one of her catchphrases on a T-shirt, she obliges. (One of her more popular phrases, "Cry havoc and let slip the dogs of civic participation," can be found on her Teespring.com store.)

Don't Lock Down All Your Content

Erin suggests that creators have at least one piece of content that is visible to the public. She says, "If I talk to my patrons about what's going on in my life, I'm going to lock that, because it's more of a conversation; if I reveal something [personal], I might lock that too. But if I'm posting a story or my work on Patreon, the vast majority of it is unlocked and free to read, because I want people to know what I have to offer."

Encourage Readers to Share Your Work

"You have to be very explicit that you want people to share your work if they like it," says Erin. "People expect it's an invasion of privacy if they're posting links to your work.

"I tell people that if you can't support, sharing is still supporting. If one person in a hundred reads the story [and] decides to subscribe, I need hundreds more people reading it. It's especially true when most of your other readers are going to be people in a creative economic bracket," says Erin.

Trust Your Patrons and Yourself

Erin says that although she has creative months, in other months, she posts only one original work. "I feel bad when I'm not doing all the things I set out to do. But I have learned to trust that the people who are supporting me are doing it because they're supporting me in what I'm doing.

"I've grown up listening to my father about the importance of direct, clear communication with clients. As long as I'm clear with [my patrons] about my limitations and what's going on, I trust that I'm not going to lose their support just because I have an off month."

Give your patrons a place to congregate. "Link a Discord server [an online chatroom] to your Patreon account, and have a place where you can chat with your patrons," Erin suggests.

THE DOS AND DON'TS OF PATREON

Patreon may be a way to earn extra money, but it can also become a source of stress. Don't let it, with the following advice in mind:

Don't Overcommit

After promising readers a bonus story in exchange for raising a certain amount of money, Erin realized what she was doing was unsustainable. "It was a recipe for burnout, because I was promising extra stories on top of the stories I was already writing in exchange for the money I needed in order to keep writing the stories."

Don't overextend yourself. It's better to keep promises (and sanity) than not.

Don't Ask Why Your Patrons Have Left

"Patreon does some sort of exit survey for the people who cancel their subscription," Erin says. "I never look at them. To me, that's a giant source of anxiety. I just ignore how many people I lose and not wonder why. It helps me keep looking forward. I'm more focused on the people who are there than chasing after the ones who leave."

OTHER PATREON TIPS

Do you want to reward your high-tier patrons? Patreon has a program called Merch for Membership for its pro and premium members. Thanks to Merch for Membership, you can reward your patrons with your very own stickers, mugs, posters, tote bags, T-shirts, and hoodies.

Best of all, Patreon will handle the shipping for you. At the time of writing, it costs $5.60 to create and ship a sticker. Patreon recommends giving stickers for patrons at the $12.00/month or higher tier. Look into suggestions for tiers and rewards on its Creators Resources page.

OTHER SOURCES OF INCOME

You don't have to limit your earnings to a single platform. When you're successful enough, diversify your income streams. Because one site can shut down your channel at any time, consider spreading your work across multiple platforms as a safety net against loss of income.

YOUTUBE

For some geektrepreneurs, YouTube *is* their creative work, where they produce such fare as TV recaps, videogame walkthroughs, board game tutorials, fan films, etc. A handful of people earn millions of dollars a year thanks to the platform. But according to a 2018 study reported in "Why Almost No One Is Making a Living on YouTube," only the top 3.5 percent of YouTubers earn $16,000 a year or more (*www.washingtonpost.com*).

Making a living solely as a YouTuber isn't impossible. It's just unlikely. But you might want to consider making YouTube an extension of your work. With thirty million people viewing YouTube every day, a video highlighting your talent—for example, creating character paintings of a customer's videogame avatar—can help your customers get to know you and act as advertising for your business.

Either record yourself while you work or photograph your work and add a voiceover explaining your process. Don't forget to put a link to your website/social media/Etsy store on your YouTube "About" page. For more help making videos and marketing them, visit YouTube's self-help channel, Creator Academy.

UPLOAD YOUR PODCAST TO YOUTUBE

Although this advice sounds like a contradiction, given that videos are a visual medium and podcasting is audio only, podcasters can make money on the video-streaming site.

Jennifer Wilson of Radio Westeros (*A Song of Ice and Fire* podcast, *https://radiowesteros.com*) says Radio Westeros frequently uploads its audio with little more than a simple backdrop. By simply giving a podcast audience another way to listen, Radio Westeros has, at the time of writing, 13,000 YouTube subscribers.

Get a "Channel Membership"

To earn income from YouTube, you need to apply to the YouTube Partner Program. To qualify, you need 1,000 subscribers who have watched 4,000 hours of your work in the last twelve months. But the real earning opportunities come at 30,000 subscribers, thanks to "channel memberships." (Exception: Gaming channels require only 1,000 subscribers.)

YouTube's channel memberships allow fans to contribute to you directly. In exchange for a viewer's monthly contribution (in the U.S., $4.99 or more, of which you receive 70 percent), you can offer your fans early access to content, exclusive content, a members-only Discord channel, or any other perk you find relevant to your work. Channel members can also apply to YouTube's BrandConnect program, which provides opportunities for you to become an influencer by connecting you directly with advertisers.

In addition, YouTube lets you sell merchandise, such as shirts, mugs, and tote bags, on your channel. Create a store on Shopify or Teespring and link it to your YouTube account.

The Dark Side of YouTube

If you create a video about how to make a pillow that resembles a beloved video-game character, be warned: the original IP owner could have the video removed for copyright infringement. To protect yourself and your content, avoid images that use someone else's IP.

While you're at it, avoid someone else's music. Make your own, use one of a dozen free music libraries online, or **hire a geeky musician**.

Even if you take precautions, any person on YouTube can frivolously—or even maliciously—lodge a complaint against you, and YouTube is obliged to make your video unavailable. While YouTube investigates a complaint, your video can't be seen by the public and is therefore not earning money (a.k.a. it is "demonetized").

You can appeal to have your video restored, but YouTube restores only one-fifth of them (see "YouTube Rarely Reinstates Removed Videos—Even When Creators Appeal," *www.theverge.com*). With this in mind, keep your videos on your own server. That way, you won't lose your work if YouTube takes it down.

Just as bad, YouTubers have been known to steal work outright by uploading *your* video to their sites and perhaps dubbing in their voices. Prove that your content is yours by adding a digital watermark of your logo in one of the corners. Watermarking makes it harder for anyone to steal your content outright and also reinforces your branding.

Case Study: Frontline Gaming Extends Its Reach with YouTube

Reece Robbins, co-owner of Frontline Gaming, runs a gaming store in a small town. He realized that "we needed to lean into the internet to have any chance of surviving." Frontline Gaming needed to differentiate itself digitally as well. "In the online marketplace, we were selling the exact same product that everybody else was selling. We needed to come up with a way to make people want to buy from us."

The solution? The entire team at Frontline Gaming—who Robbins describes as "hyper-focused subject matter experts"—contributed to growing the store's popularity daily. While some wrote articles, others took to the camera for its YouTube channel. "We were just pumping out as much content as possible," says Robbins.

Frontline Gaming's YouTube channel became a trove of *Warhammer 40,000* knowledge. "We get people excited to play the games and come to events." With 23,000 followers at the time of writing, Frontline Gaming's YouTube channel is a small but sure success.

"By a mile, [having a YouTube channel] was the best thing we did to grow the company. Without question," says Robbins. Robbins credits the YouTube channel's success to consistency. "A lot of people produce content for a couple of weeks and then drop off. But we're like clockwork."

In the videos, Robbins and his partner stand in front of two microphones and a simple backdrop—an inexpensive, simple setup. Editing is minimal. They prove you don't need money to make a successful YouTube channel. You just need to be (1) helpful and (2) consistent.

Affiliate Links

Affiliate links are links that you put in your website, social media pages, or YouTube channel that pay you a small commission every time someone purchases an item through that link. You can earn between 4 and 10 percent of the cost of the item. It's not much, but it's income that requires almost no extra work on your part, and the money adds up.

The best-known affiliate program is Amazon Associates. It's simple to start and simple to use. Best of all, you can link to any product that you want. Ask your customers/patrons/fans to purchase an item through your affiliate link rather than find what they need directly on Amazon.

Don't like the House That Bezos Built? There are multiple affiliate sites across the internet, each with different commission rates.

Advertising: Websites and Podcasts

If you have a reasonably well-trafficked website—for example, you blog about videogames or anime—you can earn income from advertising via services like AdSense, AdThrive, Monumetric, MediaNet, Mediavine, and others. You will need a minimum number of unique pageviews per month, typically 10,000.

Podcasters have their own advertising networks. David Barr Kirtley from *Geek's Guide to the Galaxy* podcast (*https://geeksguideshow.com*) says, "Most of our ads originally came from Podtrac." Another way to monetize your podcast is to join a podcast network, where you produce the content and the network finds the advertisers for you. You need a minimum audience of 5,000 listeners per month.

TWITCH STREAMING

Twitch.tv is a streaming platform where you can do whatever it is you love—live and in front of an audience. People stream themselves knitting, writing, woodworking, and playing music, and chatting with viewers is part of the fun. But for the most part, Twitch is a place where videogamers, and the people who love to watch them kill, congregate.

Advertisers who see the immediacy of the platform have taken notice. Because of this, there are monetization channels aimed directly at Twitch streamers. As with YouTube, you need to apply to the Twitch Partner Program (*www.twitch.tv*) to start earning; unlike YouTube, the Twitch requirements are less onerous. You need to have streamed five hundred minutes, have seven unique broadcasts, and an average of three or more concurrent viewers, all within the last thirty days. In addition, you need fifty or more followers.

DIRECT PAYMENTS

Streamline your donations by placing a direct link to PayPal or another payment system on your website and/or social media. As suggested by writer Alexandra Erin, remind your followers that you accept tips.

KO-FI

Micropayment site Ko-fi acts as a virtual tip jar, a good alternative to those who don't want the commitment of a Patreon account. Ko-fi one-ups Patreon by letting fans commission pieces from you directly from its site. Ko-fi also features writers, artists, and cosplayers on its main page. But it's not nearly as trafficked as Patreon, and Ko-fi has yet to offer statistics on artists' earnings on its platform. When it comes to payment systems, no news is bad news.

Gig Sites: Fiverr, Upwork, and Others

Platforms like Fiverr and Upwork are portals for gig workers to find clients. While these gig sites mainly cater to nongeeky professionals, geeks offer their skills on these sites too. For example, on Fiverr, there are professional video-game coaches and figurine painters, while Upwork's workers include comic book artists and 2D game asset designers. Other gig sites include Freelancer, FlexJobs, and 99designs.

Other Sources of Financial Support

Chris McLennan (Phoenix FearCon, film festival, *https://phoenixfearcon.com*) has been running a horror film festival and expo since 2006. Here are some money-saving tips she's picked up along the way.

Acquire Sponsorships

McLennan runs Phoenix FearCon through the largesse of sponsors, who pay for promotion [see "Case Study: How Chris McLennan's Phoenix FearCon Lost $115,000," p. 177.].

"We reach out to companies that we think would be interested, that would benefit from our target audience." Sponsors included local stores that "let us put our posters in all of their stores, and their employees put our little postcard flyers in [a bag] of anybody who went there for shopping." Not everyone responds to her request for sponsorship, but "sometimes they do."

Make sure you reach out to sponsors who are on brand; for example, McLennan found a patron in *Fangoria* magazine.

Negotiate with Event Spaces

McLennan initially ran Phoenix FearCon out of an art gallery, and later, a movie theater. But she didn't pay for the art gallery or the movie theater she rented, nor did attendees pay in tickets. Instead, the owners of the gallery and the theater were paid in "guarantees."

Some spaces will rent you a space if you "guarantee" a certain number of attendees, who will buy food and drinks. If you guarantee $5,000, and your attendees buy only $3,000 worth of food and drinks, you will have to pay the $2,000 difference to the space. If attendees spend $6,000, the profit is yours (minus taxes and expenses; if these expenses include merch, the cost of the merch can be deducted from the gross revenue).

McLennan's events were well attended, so she never had to pay the difference.

DIP INTO YOUR DAY JOB

During the week, McLennan works for a television studio. The studio gives her a discount when she rents the space for Phoenix FearCon.

McLennan isn't the only person to leverage their day job for geek work. One editor worked for a book publishing company by day. By night, they ran a small-press magazine from their publisher's office.

THE PROS AND CONS OF CONS

Conventions are a melting pot of ideas and thoughts, and
people wait all year just to have their voices heard.

—*Daniel Delgado, vendor*

Conventions, which are the highlight of geeky social calendars worldwide, are
a one-stop shop for everything fabulous in fandom. Meeting your geek heroes.
Attending thought-provoking panels. Advanced screenings. Cosplay, cosplay,
cosplay. And, of course, the dealer's room. For attendees, conventions mean fun.

For vendors, conventions mean work. If you think that you can experience
the whole convention while working, think again. Selling can be an exhausting
experience, even before the con begins. Also, if you work at a convention, you're
turning your vacation from the real world into a place of business. Do you really
want to do that to yourself?

If you're serious about your geeky venture, read on.

CONVENTIONS BY THE NUMBERS

Conventions aren't just a place to sell your wares. They're fabulous opportunities to grow your business. In the pre-pandemic Before Times, over one million people attended geeky conventions each year. That's one million people in your target audience, all in the same space together.

Here's a roundup of some popular American cons (most recent numbers, 2017).*

*Note: Not all conventions keep records on attendance (like Penny Arcade Expo), and not all conventions have published their figures (like WonderCon, D23, and Wizard World), so tack on at least 100,000 to that total.

Anime Expo:	100,000
Awesome Con:	70,000
Chicago Comic Entertainment Expo:	80,000
Denver Pop Culture Con:	115,000
Dragon Con:	80,000
Emerald City Comic Con:	91,000
GenCon:	60,000
L.A. Comic Con:	100,000
New York Comic Con:	180,000
Otakon:	25,000
Phoenix Fan Fusion:	80,000
San Diego Comic-Con:	130,000
TOTAL:	**1,111,000**

If you had attended these twelve conventions, an average of one a month, you had potentially over one million opportunities to make a sale.

Had. At the time of writing, conventions are virtual spaces. But they won't remain that way forever. Conventions like Dragon Con are planned for a year in advance by fans who love to surround themselves with people like them. People who really care about having comic books that are graded 9.0 and higher. It may take a few years, but conventions and convention culture will blossom again.

RENAISSANCE FAIRES AND THE SOCIETY FOR CREATIVE ANACHRONISM (SCA)

RenFaires are outdoor fairs that encourage participants—and require vendors—to dress in Renaissance garb. If your goods are fantasy inspired, rather than sci-fi, consider applying for a booth. You will be required to commit to the weekends that the Faire is open, as many as thirteen.

The SCA *(www.sca.org)* is an historical recreation group that recreates the more appealing/less plague-ridden aspects of life in the years 600–1600. Attend a local event and see for yourself that most members are also convention attendees. If you plan to merchant, your wares must fit in with the historic themes; think goods made of wood, leather, metal, etc.

Why Sell at a Convention

Selling your goods at a convention can be good for your wallet. It's also good for your business in general. Here's how.

It's an Opportunity to Network

Although you can build a fandom from behind a keyboard, conventions are places where people get to meet the real you. Your attitude. Your experience. Your enthusiasm. When you meet people in person, you automatically develop a relationship with them.

In "The Science of When You Need In-Person Communication," Fast Company writes that the more that someone sees you, the more likable you become (*www.fastcompany.com*). This agreeability is important, because you're selling yourself as much as you are a product.

You Get Creative

Daniel Delgado of Altruistic (costume weapons, home decor, *www.alltru2u.com*) says that speaking with fans helps him envision concepts for his future items. "I get better ideas from crappier shows, because you have more time to talk to people. If I'm not going to get money from the show, I'm going to get a money-making idea from the show."

As an example, Delgado said a customer-requested scythe, styled on one wielded on *Buffy the Vampire Slayer*, has become a reliable seller.

You Meet Other Vendors

Other vendors are your allies, even if they sell the same products you do. Here is a chance to learn from them. Introduce yourself. Be polite and helpful. And when they have a spare moment, ask questions. They will tell you which shows they've been burned at and which shows are worth their weight in latinum.

Just as important, some vendors will become your friends; after all, you already have a great deal in common with them. Seeing a friendly face at the loading dock will ease your hard work, if only a little.

You Get Your Finger on the Pulse

Even if your chats with fans are limited, you still get an eyeful of information. You see which characters and media are popular, based on cosplay, T-shirts, and other wearables. If you notice that fans are cosplaying the most recent Disney character, and your stock doesn't include that character, you might want to rectify this gap in your inventory.

You Get to Sell Your Wares

You're there to make money. And in some cases, conventions are *the* best place to sell your items. For example, clothing is more appealing when potential buyers can try on items and be assured they fit.

CONSIDER VOLUNTEERING

Before you dive into selling at a convention, consider volunteering at another vendor's booth. This opportunity may give you a better sense of what to expect.

Bonus points if you can manage to speak on a panel, where your knowledge translates into visibility, which translates into free advertising.

You Get an Ego Boost

Delgado says that selling his work at conventions "is a boost of self-confidence you can't get anywhere."

Laura Rosado of Popcycled Baubles (geeky housewares and personal items, *https://popcycledbaubles.com*) agrees. "People I see year after year stop by and say hello. Even if they don't buy anything, they always bring friends, and their friends buy things. Those are experiences that are validating and amazing."

When fans like your work, they will straight-up tell you. This means you're not just getting paid in cash: you're getting paid in ego.

WHICH CONVENTION SHOULD YOU ATTEND?

As a fan, you know which shows you love. But as a vendor, you have other decisions to make. Here are some important facets to consider when determining to which convention you want to submit a vendor application.

THE CONVENTION'S THEME

If you specialize in pencil sketches of anime characters, your work might not sell well at a geographically desirable yet thematically incompatible horror convention. If you base your work solely on your favorite television show, when a nearby convention celebrates a collectible card game, foot traffic will just keep walking.

The good news is, there are conventions for every geeky strain, from comic books, videogames, tabletop games, anime, books, media, and furry fandom. Geek culture is so expansive that you can always find your subculture. Even your *sub*-subculture.

THE GUEST LIST

As Greg Topalian, the creator of New York Comic Con and CEO of Left Field Media, says, "Programming is great, but the celebrity piece [of the convention] is a once-in-a-lifetime experience. Access to which celebrities they're going to see, and get an autograph or photo with, can be the determining factor of why [fans] come. The bigger the celebrity, the bigger deal it is to the fan."

TAILOR YOUR MERCHANDISE

Let's say you sell clever mugs. If you're at a convention where the former stars of *Doctor Who* are speaking, you'll want to bring your *Doctor Who*-themed mugs. In addition, you'll want to carry mugs from other UK shows or shows where British actors are more prominent. If one of the stars of *Doctor Who* also appeared in a geeky movie, you'll want to bring a mug related to that film as well.

Your *World of Warcraft* mugs might sell at that convention too—but display your *Doctor Who* work more prominently.

THE LOCATION OF THE CONVENTION

Delgado chose the location of his first convention because of its proximity to his sister's home, where he could stay for free. If you can't find a friendly crash pad, hotels or Airbnbs are an unavoidable cost of doing business.

And then there's the time and expense of travel, particularly flying. As Rosado says of flying to conventions as a vendor, "I will never do that again." Although Rosado sold much of her stock at this busy convention, she says that her costs—which included airplane tickets for her and her husband; booth fee; and outlays of shipping her stock, renting a room, and paying for food and taxis—"were so high that making it back was almost impossible."

TRAVEL TIME

Before you venture afield, keep in mind that travel time means wear and tear on your vehicle. More than that, you need to consider time away from your actual work. Delgado says, "The more I'm on the road, the less product I can make."

THE AGE OF THE CONVENTION

Author Russell Nohelty (*www.russellnohelty.com*), who has attended one hundred conventions in three years, says the first year of a convention's existence is a good year to sell your wares. The convention committee tends to advertise a show heavily in its first year, to draw in large crowds.

"I will not do a second-year show," says Nohelty, who has seen some conventions' attendance drop by half that of its first year. "Once a show is in its fourth year, I know it's stable or growing." He prefers to table at shows that have been running more than ten years.

THE REPUTATION OF THE CONVENTION

There's a reason you need to consider the convention's reputation. Topalian says that, because of the popularity of convention culture, new conventions are frequently springing up. "Not all of them are ready for the kinds of fiscal and organizing responsibilities that come at an event like this," says Topalian.

The reputation of the promoter is also important, as conventions live and die by the competency of the people running then. Talk to fellow vendors, and search online for postconvention chat. If one vendor states you should avoid a convention or a promoter, that's not enough data; if dozens of vendors do, then you may want to consider other shows.

Case Study: Spat Oktan Accidentally Becomes a Convention Showrunner

Spat Oktan, who runs the Spatcave page on Etsy, didn't set out to become a convention showrunner.

Oktan and his friends—Creation Convention veterans—tried to attend a Chiller Convention when they were stymied by an overlong queue. They decided to wait out the crowd at a nearby bar.

Oktan says, "One of the people running security saw us, remembered us from other shows, and said, 'Do you guys want to work? We're short handed.' So next thing we knew, we were behind the scenes, working with the actors, escorting them places, and controlling lines. It was crazy."

One celebrity guest spent his time at his table getting drunk. "It was a trial by fire," says Oktan.

In 2006, Oktan attended Big Apple Comic Con, then decided he wanted to get a table at the next year's show. (Oktan is also a makeup artist and propmaker.) He approached an operational manager for a chat, and . . .

"Literally, by the end of that night, I was running part of the floor, and I don't even know how it happened," Oktan says.

After a fast-paced day, he had planned to go home. But then he passed by a map that the convention organizers had laid out for the next day's autograph signings. "I looked at it, and in two seconds, I just said, 'That's not gonna work. Your exit line crosses your entry line, and you're gonna create a bottleneck.'"

The convention's organizers asked Oktan how he would lay out the floorplan differently. They liked his idea enough to say, "Great. Get here tomorrow morning and set that up."

"And I'm like, 'I don't work here,'" he says. The convention's organizer responded, "Oh, you do now."

Since then, Oktan has helped run several Big Apple Comic Cons and multiple Wizard World cons. In years without pandemics, he runs Eternal Con and Winter Con.

[For more on running a convention, see chapter 7, "Get a Geeky Job," p. 153.]

The Length of the Convention

Conventions range from one-day shows to four-day events. Delgado says that he prefers one-day conventions because their table fees are lower than weekend-long affairs. In addition, he avoids one-day shows that have expanded into weekend shows because they cost twice as much yet don't always attract twice the audience.

If it takes hours to set up your booth and displays, you may prefer those longer shows.

The Foot Traffic

It's simple math: The more attendees at a show, the more attendees you may attract. Accordingly, Scott Wolpow of Family Dragon (dragon-themed art and figurines, *FamilyDragon.com*) says that he will sell only at conventions with 5,000 attendees or more.

However, population doesn't always translate into sales. Although the Flowertown Festival in Summerville, South Carolina, draws up to 200,000 "regular joes" over three days, Delgado says that his geeky woodworking sells better at small comic book conventions frequented by geeks.

The Competition

Do you sell handmade fantasy-themed tarot decks? Will the convention be attended by five other tarot deck sellers? If so, you might not earn back your fees, let alone make a profit.

Sunshine Levy of GinGee Girls says, "Do your homework." This includes:

 Read through the current vendor list, found online.

Research the previous year's program guide.

Ask the convention sales office how many people who sell [*insert your item here*] will be attending.

The Price of the Table/Booth

The biggest conventions—San Diego Comic-Con, New York Comic Con, and Dragon Con—will cost you the biggest bucks, while smaller, more specialized conventions won't charge you an arm, a kidney, and your second heart. Also, conventions in more densely populated urban areas will charge you more than in suburban ones.

As an example, in 2019, My Little Pony convention BronyCon, in Baltimore, Maryland, sold a 10' × 10' space for $385; this amount pays for two badges, electricity, and basic union labor. General geek con CoreCon, in Fargo, North Dakota, charges only $80; this amount gets you a space and two badges.

Check convention websites for prices and budget accordingly.

SMALLER IS BETTER

Sharpen your sales skills at a smaller con before you commit to a large one. Mitigate your risk while you learn how to be effective; then use what you've learned to hone your techniques.

Extra Costs

Some conventions have extra costs you should be aware of. Check with the exhibitor's guide in advance so that you can budget your banknotes accordingly. (No exhibitor's guide? That's not a good sign.)

Electricity

Prices vary, but you'll need electricity if you run special lighting or electronics, such as a credit card machine.

STORAGE FEES

If you're shipping in your goods from out of town, hotels and convention centers will store packages for you. For a fee, of course.

DRAYAGE FEES, A.K.A. LOADING/UNLOADING FEES

Some conventions won't allow you to haul your goods to and from your booth: their staff does the hauling for you. Expect to pay by weight. The heavier your pallet, the more you'll have to spend.

LIABILITY INSURANCE

Daniel Delgado says he uses whatever insurance the convention recommends. However, he prefers cons that don't have the requirement. He says, "In some shows, we pay $300 to $400 for insurance, on top of the booth. That's a cost you don't get back."

MINIMIZE EXPENSES BY SHARING A TABLE

Author Russell Nohelty likes to share a table.* Sharing not only trims costs but also gives you an instant partner. Nohelty prefers to team up with writers who share a similar niche yet do not directly compete with his work. "I want [a booth partner] to fill in something that I don't have but something my ideal audience would want."

As a writer of horror comics, he prefers "people who have monster YA books or children's books, because I don't have that." To further save on expenses, Nohelty and his booth partner drive to the convention together and split the cost of gas and parking.

*Note: Some conventions have a no-sharing policy.

How to Ace Your Vendor Application

To sell at a convention, you can't just pay your booth fee and walk in. No, you need to apply for the privilege of paying your booth fee. You may even be rejected. Keep the following tips in mind when filling out your application.

Be Unique

Conventions and the fans who love them want to see diversity in the dealer's room, because variety is the spice of the convention. What makes your business stand out? A convention that has given the go-ahead to twenty other comic book dealers may reject you if you sell only current issues. Narrow your focus to only 1960s to 1970s horror comics, and you may have yourself a space. To repeat, if your product isn't unique, you will be rejected.

Read the Vendor Guidelines

Before you apply, read the vendor guidelines, which you can find either on a convention's website or by reaching out to the online contact person. Reading them is important because the guidelines spell out exactly what a convention *isn't* looking for.

For example, the Heroes & Villains Fan Fest guidelines include a list of items it won't permit you to sell. Weapons. Vaping accessories. Food and beverages, unless they come prepackaged (no samples, either). And weirdly, vacation and timeshare giveaways.

Do you have insurance and specialized permits so that you can legally sell those snacks? It's great that you thought of that . . . but you'll still have to find a different convention.

No Bootlegging

In conventions past, repackaging someone else's IP and selling it as your own (think crudely duplicated DVDs) were a staple. However, modern cons are less eager to attract the ire of big-name, lawyered-up IP owners—particularly because IP holders now attend conventions.

Topalian says if his team sees bootlegged goods, "We try to work it out in an amicable way. We tell them they need to take these down and sell only products that are not bootlegged. If they don't, we make it clear that if they continue to do that, we will close down their booth.

"We have had to do it," says Topalian. "It's not fun."

BUILD YOUR INVENTORY IN ADVANCE

Building your inventory takes time, money, and dedication. Lucky for the customers of PopCycled Baubles, Laura Rosado has all three. Gaze upon her organizational skills, ye mighty, and despair.

Rosado starts by considering "what product lines I want to remove." If items have underperformed—say, her Avengers lanyards—"I put them in a $5 bin to clear them out."

"I think about the new items I want to add," says Rosado. In some cases, she bulks out her existing products; in other cases, she adds a new product line, such as upcycled coasters.

Rosado then orders the supplies she needs to make them. For example, if she's selling fabric-wrapped flasks, she needs to order flasks, fabric, fabric glue, and spray to make the fabric water resistant. She also needs paper, to print out instructions on how to care for her flasks.

Next, she creates a to-do list of items she needs to make.

Rosado then tracks her time during the workweek, "so I can stay on task. I check things off as I go through, and that gets me through my to-do list in small chunks. I get to work building stock, and I just build and build."

WHAT MERCH DO YOU MAKE FOR A CONVENTION?

What do you make for a convention? Old and trusted or the new hotness?

If you say "the new hotness," not so fast. Rosado says, "The characters that are hot right now because of a movie is a fleeting desire for the buyer. Sometimes [timing your products to a movie release] works, sometimes it doesn't. I don't go overboard making things specific to that movie. Honestly, I have found that icons stay icons, and fans are still more swayed by those iconic characters, like Batman, Wonder Woman, and Spider-Man."

BUILD YOUR BOOTH OR TABLE IN ADVANCE

Before the convention, section out the space you've rented—typically 6' × 8 ' or 10' × 10'—at home. Then place your items the way you plan to have them displayed at the convention so you can see what fits and what looks good. If your display doesn't attract the eye as much as you had hoped, you can start from scratch in the comfort of your home, not the chaos of the show floor.

Consider the height of your booth too. Although you might want a taller grid wall to fit more merch, you can anticipate a height limitation of 7' or 8' tall. Bring a sturdy chair or stepladder to reach those out-of-reach items. Also, place heavier items at arm's height or lower, to prevent injuries when pulling an item down from a high shelf.

THE COST(S) OF DOING BUSINESS

There are some surprising costs to selling your goods. Let's look at some expenditures you'll have to expend.*

*Note: Not all of these expenses will apply to you, and some of these purchases are one-time expenses. But make sure to include the relevant parts in your budget.

THE BOOTH SPACE

As a vendor, you should apply to a convention as soon as the application is available so that you have more options when it comes to the location of your table or booth. While attending a convention, Rosado books next year's booth space. And instead of putting down a typical 30 percent reservation fee, she pays 100 percent in advance. That way, she doesn't need to budget for that cost during the coming year. However, some conventions don't have advanced booking, and others make you reapply every single year.

THE HOTEL (AND/OR AIRPLANE TICKETS, IF NEEDED)

After a long day of slaving over a hot dealer table, some vendors choose an Airbnb or crash at the pad of a local friend. Others prefer hotels, which are more expensive but provide both networking opportunities with fans and points for loyalty programs. These points add up to the occasional free room or upgrade to a suite.

Book well in advance for mega-cons such as San Diego Comic-Con, as these rooms are filled with Flash-like speed.

DISPLAY ITEMS

Conventions tend to provide only a table and two chairs, so you'll need to provide shelving, grid walls, cases, a backdrop, a tablecloth, clips to hang items, and/or book/magazine stands—everything you need to best display your wares. Some vendors who don't display items or have a small amount of material to sell (say, copies of a single book) recommend retractable pop-up stands to make the booth feel more full.

A CLIPBOARD, PAPER, AND PENS

Having a clipboard, paper, and pens is critical, as this is how you acquire the email addresses of people who drop by your booth. Using these tools is how you build your all-important mailing list [see "Build a Mailing List," p. 89.].

WAYS TO CONTACT YOU

There are two ways for potential customers to contact you:

Business cards and flyers: These are simple yet effective ways for potential customers to reach you, although a good printing job costs coin of the realm.

QR codes: These boxy links send viewers to your website or wherever you do business, and best of all, you can acquire one for free. But Wi-Fi reception at conventions can be spotty.

Use both, for the best of both worlds.

A CELL-PHONE-BASED CREDIT CARD READER (AND PORTABLE POWER PACK)

Convention centers and hotels sometimes charge vendors for electricity. But if the only reason to have electricity is to run a credit card machine, there's a good workaround: Willow Volante uses reader attachments on her cell phones and tablets to allow them to accept credit cards. "If your phone holds ten hours of battery, you should be fine," Volante says.

Volante makes sure her phone will hold a charge by buying a new phone every year. To her, this is a money-saving business expense. "If you think about it, the cost of a new iPhone is $700, and paying for the electricity is $150 a day. So in two shows, it's worth the cost of an iPhone every year."

Get more life out of your old phone with a power pack. Don't forget to charge it too.

A Point-of-Sales System

Point-of-sales systems like Square, Shopify, or Vend will process your payments for a small transaction fee—in addition to the fees that your credit card charges. These systems will also help you track your inventory.

If you accept cash, remember to bring dollar bills and coins for change.

Oh Look, Even More Costs

A dolly: Rosado says that although convention centers typically provide them, you may have to wait for your wheels when you're loading in. Having your own dolly saves you time and therefore stress.

Boxes and bins to transport your goods: Rosado recommends clear plastic boxes so you can see at a glance what material goes in which box. Hardcore convention veterans number their boxes so they know what to pack and unpack and in what order.

Bags for sold items: If you sell fragile items, you'll also need to buy boxes and packing materials. You don't want your new fans to be as crushed as the item they purchased.

> ## INVEST IN HAND SANITIZER
>
> Even before COVID-19, attendees ran the risk of "con crud"—that is, the cold you picked up during a con. If customers touch your items, offer them hand sanitizer. They, and you, may feel more comfortable.

Parking fees: If you drive to the convention, you have to park your vehicle somewhere. The larger your vehicle, the steeper the fee.

Pro tip, via Scott Wolpow: For conventions in New York City, where parking is expensive, he rents a van near his home and drops it off at a location near the con. After the con, he rents another van in the city and drops it off near his home. This way, he avoids paying parking fees.

WHAT TO PACK FOR THE CONVENTION

Don't forget to bring your suitcase, as Rosado almost has . . . more than once. Also, be sure to bring

 Protein snacks, bottles (and more bottles) of water, aspirin, and your meds.

Food for a specialized diet, such as gluten-free. Bringing your own food will save you stress wondering if you can find a meal at the convention center.

A thin shirt, plus a sweater or light jacket. You never know if you'll be placed near an air conditioner or a full-blast heater.

Ear plugs. You never know if you'll be placed next to the booth with a videogame display that plays its theme on repeat. On repeat. On repeat.

A cushion for your con-issued metal fold-out chair; a floor pad if you plan on standing.

The comfy shoes.

AT THE CONVENTION

All of your hard work is about to pay off—you hope. The doors are opening, the customers are beginning to mill. But selling is only part of your mission. You have other side quests to achieve.

HAVE EMOTIONAL SUPPORT IF YOU NEED IT

What if you're an introvert who finds sitting at a table in the middle of a crowd your idea of personal hell?

Bring support with you in the form of an enthusiastic, extroverted salesperson who enjoys talking with strangers to run interference for you. But if you need more than that, bring an emotional support buddy. Having both a support person and a salesperson will cut into your profits because you'll need to pay for an extra ticket. But for some, sanity is worth the cut in take-home pay.

Make sure you give your assistant(s) breaks. Even the hardest workers need personal time to fill in the gaps in their comic book collections.

GIVE "GOOD TABLE"

Allan Rosenberg, who runs Artist Alley at Big Apple Comic Con, says that he doesn't just choose artists for the quality of their work. He wants artists who "give good table." In essence, he wants people who can hold a conversation with fans who stop by. And isn't that what fans want too—someone with whom they identify and can geek out together?

Engage with fans about what you both love, and they will linger at your booth. That's one more opportunity to sell your work. You could be the world's most talented artisan, with fans who come for miles to touch the hem of your garment. But if you come across as arrogant or dismissive, you will lose that fan forever. (You also don't need people telling their friends, "Dude, that person was a @!$#.")

Showrunners also prefer artists and vendors who won't give customers a hard sell, which can make shy and/or cash-strapped attendees feel uncomfortable.

Build a Good Reputation with the Con

Conventions are a surprisingly small world, and convention showrunners know other convention showrunners . . . and they share names of vendors who have caused problems. Vendor issues include bouncing checks for table fees and leaving a mess behind.

Worse, there's taking extra time loading out your space. Showrunners—most of whom start work in the wee hours—can't leave until you've vacated. Plus, some facilities will fine the convention if you're late out the door.

Keep your rep as clean as your collectible figurines. This goes for social media too. If you start flame wars with other vendors and showrunners online, you can be pegged as a person of disinterest.

Pay Attention to Your Customers

Your customers will tell you what they like and don't like about your merchandise. Pay attention to them.

Daniel Delgado says, "People will tell you in ten seconds if they like what you have, if they've seen it before, or if they can't afford it—whether they have the words or not. You can get all that if you're paying attention."

Be Helpful but Not Too Hands-On

Sunshine Levy says, "When people walk into my booth, I say, 'Welcome to GinGee Girls. We make everything ourselves. Everything is dishwasher and microwave safe. If you have any questions, feel free to ask, and feel free to touch.' And that's it. Then I leave them alone."

Only if potential customers linger does Levy ask if she can answer any questions. To encourage patrons to buy, she tells them that if they purchase her work at the convention now, rather than online later, they won't have to pay a shipping fee.

Build Relationships

Mike Zhang, a salesperson for Angel Sword (*www.angelsword.com*) at Renaissance Faires, says that it's important to build relationships when selling expensive items. He says, "I tell people, 'It's free to look at and free to hold. It's just not free to take home' and 'I promise not to sell it to you.' It opens people up to experiencing your wares."

Zhang says, "Customers may not be able to afford them now, but fortunes change. Two years later, maybe they can." And they do. One customer who admired Angel Sword's work eventually purchased a $4,000 sword three years after first seeing it.

Make Your Table an Experience

Danielle Reichman will retie your convertible dress, so you could walk away from her booth with a completely new look—even if you purchased her dress at a different convention.

Black Phoenix Alchemy Lab (perfumery, *blackphoenixalchemylab.com* hands out samples of their geeky-themed perfumes to the curious. But first, their sellers ask fans their likes and dislikes and answer fragrance-related questions. Customers walk away from BPAL with an A+ in perfume education.

In addition to their steampunk-themed booth, Tea & Absinthe section off their inventory away from the public eye to enhance their booth's 19th-century feel.

Sell Yourself

Russell Nohelty offers "a free crappy drawing" to anyone who walks by his booth, just to engage with potential customers. He also offers a picture from his books—but to snag one, a potential customer has to sign up for his mailing list. Although people drop off his mailing list, he says, many remain.

LEVERAGE STAR POWER

Levy offers a free mug to any celebrity who walks into her booth. Why? "Because them sitting at their table with my mug while they're signing is free advertising." If the opportunity presents itself, she asks them to take a selfie and post it online. "Having them Instagram with you in your booth is huge because then their whole following suddenly becomes your following."

WHERE IS THE BEST SPACE AT THE CONVENTION?

Everyone wants a prime location for their booth: highly trafficked locations, such as near the exits or off large alleyways, where you can be seen at a distance. But what is the best location for you?

According to Greg Topalian (convention showrunner, Awesome Con), your merchandise should dictate your location. "Being near Artist Alley is a legitimate draw for comics fans. If you're a comic-oriented vendor, being near Artist Alley is a good idea. If you have movie tie-ins that attract the broader pop culture fan, I would say you would want to be placed near the autographing and photographing areas," he says.

Convention showrunner Spat Oktan believes the best location is near the bathrooms . . . because everyone walks past your booth eventually.

AFTER THE CONVENTION

After the convention, your priority is to go home, put your inventory away, and catch up on some long-needed sleep. But when you wake up, it's time to do some postconvention work.

Set Aside Money for Taxes

That money you've made isn't free and clear. Set aside the money you've earned according to your tax bracket. (You can find your tax bracket online, according to how much money you estimate you'll be earning that year.) If you put away the money now, you won't have to scramble to acquire it come tax time.

Add to Your Mailing List

Take the email/snail mail addresses that you've collected at the convention and add them to your mailing list. This is your newly updated marketing list. Use it when you have an announcement.

Look Through Your Remaining Inventory

Your card games have sold like a card game about hotcakes, but your board games only bored customers. Now is the time to produce more card games.

When to Cut a Convention from Your Calendar

Attending conventions where you lose money is bad for business, no matter how much you personally enjoy the con or the showrunner. Cut unprofitable conventions immediately.

Delgado says that, in order for him to consider the convention a success, he spends 30 percent of his earnings on logistics. For example, if he spends $100 on a table, $100 on travel, and $100 on food for a convention (total: $300) and earns $1,000 or more, he will return to that show next year. (Note that this is not $700 profit. You also have to consider the cost of inventory, as well as local and state sales tax.)

GET A GEEKY JOB

You could start a business from scratch, and everything would be yours. Your labor. Your earnings. Your debts. For some, that's too much work and too much risk.

But you can still have a job doing what you love in geek culture by getting a job with an already-established business. If you break down coveted geek culture jobs, you'll see they tend to cluster within the verticals (that is, industries) of publishing, comic books, film, gaming, and occasionally, music and fashion, and they make an excellent fit for people with an artistic bend or a technological one. The tech-centered jobs pay better, and if you have the skills, are easier to acquire. Conversely, the more creative jobs are highly competitive, and as a result, pay comparatively poorly. Let's just say you won't have many coins to toss your Witcher.

A steady creative job in geek culture is also as rare as a mint issue of *Detective Comics #27*. (It's rare in the nongeek world too, the advertising industry notwithstanding.) Just as bad, there's a lot of churn. Even if you land a job, through no fault of your own, you may not keep it for long.

But even if you don't have a *job*, you still may have a *career*. As Cindy Khoo of Scanline VFX says about the film and television industry, "A stable career is realistic and attainable for anyone good at their craft." This is also true for those who pursue every other geek vertical.

In addition, these talents can be transferable to other geek verticals. For example, artists can draw comic books, board game art, book covers, etc.; writers can write books, short stories, plays, movies, and articles; digital artists can work in film effects and videogame art.

Here's a look at some geeky jobs in geeky industries, with advice on how to get yourself hired.

FILM AND TELEVISION

Acording to "New Data: The American Film and Television Industry Continues to Drive Economic Growth in All 50 States," before the pandemic, the film and television industry "support[ed] 2.6 million jobs, pa[id] out $177 billion in total wages, and comprise[d] over 93,000 businesses" (*www.motionpictures.org*). COVID-19 took a scythe to those numbers. But even a pandemic has proven that, although access to a movie theater is desirable, it's not at all necessary to enjoy content. Streaming services now offer new releases of films, where viewers can enjoy them at home, in the comfort of their Hobbit-foot slippers.

The television industry in particular is blossoming, thanks to multiple streaming services that are providing their own unique content. This growth has led to innovations in filmmaking, such as Disney's masterwork, the Volume, a dome of LED screens 75 feet in diameter, which displays any background the visual effects artists can dream up. As a result, big-budget filmmakers will be relying on technology even more than they currently do—and relying less on traditional jobs such as transportation, location scouting, and set building.

Still, if you say you want to work in film, there's a plethora of jobs to choose from. They include director (controlling the action on screen), producer (hiring the talent, acquiring the funding or the IP), set designer (someone who advises on the objects seen on screen), gaffer (a funny, funny word for *electrician*), and so much more.

CINDY KHOO, SCANLINE VFX

Cindy Khoo is the Global Head of Production/Executive Producer for Asia for Scanline VFX, an award-winning visual effects studio. You can thank her and Scanline for the fiery destruction of King's Landing in the final season of *Game of Thrones*. Before she helped Drogon take wing, Khoo started her career as an intern.

THERE'S MORE STABILITY IN POSTPRODUCTION THAN IN PRODUCTION

Although production jobs fold when filming wraps, Khoo has found herself gainfully employed in the field of postproduction, that is, the work that takes place after the actors exit stage left.

Postproduction jobs can be temporary too. But some postproduction companies "offer longer contracts that are not tied to a particular project," says Khoo. Because of this, some postproduction crew can keep their job for years.

WORK IS MORE IMPORTANT THAN SCHOOL, BUT . . .

Khoo credits the part-time film work she did during college, rather than getting a university degree, for helping her obtain a job. But Khoo's time at school helped her in one important way: she learned about jobs from fellow classmates. "There's always a lot of opportunities around you there," says Khoo.

Knowing the Right Software Is Helpful, But . . .

The visual effects industry relies on software, for example, Shotgun (a production-focused organization tool, similar to Trello), while people in more technical roles need expertise in their industry-standard tooling. That's the easy part, says Khoo. "Learning software, it's not rocket science."

Because all software becomes outdated eventually, Khoo says, "It's important to know what's new now and what's the next thing we should be doing." She believes that "constant curiosity and then learning what you don't know" is more valuable than knowing one type of software.

Don't Be Picky About Your First Jobs

"The most important thing is to not be picky about a job" when you're beginning your career, says Khoo. If you had hoped for a job in lighting but are offered a job as a production assistant—typically, the lowest rung on the film/television ladder—you should take the PA job. And like it.

Build experience, so you can prove yourself and then branch out—Khoo started off in sound editing—but unless you have the first job, there's nowhere to branch out *from*.

There Really Is a Job for Everyone

The film and television industry needs artists, technicians, and everyone in between. People are needed to build sets, move fragile equipment, and ensure that the actor's drink has only three ice cubes in every shot. Film sets also require the skills of noncreative professionals, such as accountants and nurses.

Despite the glamour and prestige that surrounds the film industry, the day-to-day work can be far from exciting, as anyone who has digitally erased a moustache can tell you.

FASHION

The fashion industry has been taking geek culture seriously the last decade, what with collaborations between *Jurassic Park* and Dolce & Gabbana; Catwoman and the Blonds; *Star Wars* and Rodarte; and *Tron: Legacy* and a variety of designers. There are currently no major fashion brands dedicated to haute couture (although Ashley Eckstein, who owns female-centered geeky clothier Her Universe, throws a geek-centric fashion competition each year at San Diego Comic-Con). However, smaller companies like Her Universe, Hot Topic, and Torrid make geekwear for the mass market. These brands hire designers, albeit infrequently.

If you're a geeky designer, you may use your powers of persuasion to convince your fashion label to create a dedicated geek branch. You could win the Her Universe fashion show, whose prize is an opportunity to design a collection. Or you could just start your own label, like Eckstein.

WRITING / PUBLISHING

There will always be geeky readers for writers of fantastical, imaginative tales. And they will choose books and stories with unicorns, spaceships, and zombies over books without them . . . every day of the week and twice on Life Day.

Writing science fiction, fantasy, and horror novels and stories may earn you a beloved fan base and acclaim from your peers, but rarely does it garner a full-time living. As former president of the Science Fiction & Fantasy Writers of America (SFWA) Jane Jewell said in 2006, only between fifty and one hundred genre authors earned a living (see "Don't Quit Your Day Job: The Financial Reality of Writing Science Fiction and Fantasy," *www.intergalacticmedicine show.com*).

After a steep decline of print sales in 2019, down to 693.7 million (see "Print Unit Sales Fell 1.3% in 2019," *www.publishersweekly.com*), genre fiction print sales rocketed to 750.9 million (see "Print Book Sales Rose 8.2% in 2020," *www.publishersweekly.com*), thanks to a boost from the pandemic.

In addition to the traditional publishers like Tor, Baen, Angry Robot, or smaller presses like Small Beer and Subterranean, self-publishing is easier than ever. Companies like Amazon's Kindle Direct Publishing, Apple Books, and Barnes & Noble Direct Press offer easy paths to digital publishing, and businesses like Lulu and IngramSpark can help you put that book directly into your hands.

Self-publishing lacks editorial oversight, so **hire a geeky copy editor** to polish your prose.

Writers aren't limited to fiction. Geeky nonfiction writing includes collections of critical essays or biographies of a favorite author. Plus, anyone with an opinion can turn their know-it-all-ness into online commentary. If you have ever argued that *Star Trek* is better than *Star Wars* or DC is better than Marvel (and, of course, you have), you have a potential gig as an article writer in the making . . . just not a lucrative one.

JOHN JOSEPH ADAMS, LIGHTSPEED MAGAZINE

John Joseph Adams (*www.johnjosephadams.com*) started publishing life as an editor at *The Magazine of Fantasy & Science Fiction* and later became the editor and publisher of *Lightspeed* magazine. He even had his own imprint at Houghton Mifflin Harcourt: John Joseph Adams Books.

Adams has the following tips for writers and editors who know the winners of the Quidditch World Cup but not the FIFA World Cup.

HAUNT JOB BOARDS

Find a job on general sites like Monster and Indeed, as well as specialized sites like Publisher's Weekly and Publisher's Marketplace, says Adams. "I just sent out resumes. Basically, that's how you get a job in publishing."

But the field of science fiction, fantasy, and horror is a relatively small slice of the publishing pie. "You're gonna have to really haunt those job boards and jump on those opportunities whenever they open up, because there's always going to be a lot of applicants," says Adams.

FOLLOW EDITORS AND WRITERS ON SOCIAL MEDIA

Follow your favorite editors on their social media sites (typically Twitter) "because they post editorial jobs that open up within their companies." Follow popular writers too, as they retweet editors, which gives you another opportunity to see their posts.

KNOW YOU'RE GOING TO BE STRAPPED FOR CASH

Although there are publishers in every major city, "If you want to work in editorial, the New York area is basically your best bet," says Adams. "Unfortunately, it's hard to live there, because the salaries aren't going to be that big when you first start."

The publishing industry usually requires its employees to start at the lowliest of positions: editorial assistant. Despite the fabulous perks—meeting your favorite authors; snagging copies of books well in advance of the public; being surrounded by words and the people who love them—it's poorly paid work that requires long hours.

Adams notes that the salaries aren't much better in the more senior positions either.

ATTEND CONVENTIONS / READINGS / PROFESSIONAL GATHERINGS

When not in the grip of a pandemic, Adams recommends attending literary conventions such as Readercon (Boston area) and the World Fantasy Convention (locations vary) "because all sorts of publishing professionals go to these things."

If an editor from a publishing house that you admire will be attending, "Find out what books they've edited. Just in case you end up in a conversation with them, you'll know who you're talking to," says Adams. And when you do speak, be on your best behavior. "Be a normal person and not slime all over editors when you meet them and become a nuisance."

In addition, many cities have reading series and science fiction literary societies. Attending them means you'll be meeting your favorite current authors. Your future favorites too.

Keep Up on Current Books

Adams says, "Read, read, read." For writers and editors, reading your favorite authors teaches you what makes their work *work*.

It's not enough to know the classics: you need to keep up with current trends. For example, says Adams, "If you haven't read Nora Jemisin [author of *The Broken Earth* series], and if you want to get a job in publishing, you need to be reading Nora Jemisin." (And if you don't know who she is, she's a MacArthur Foundation Genius Grant winner and the first person to win three consecutive Hugo Awards.)

Visit the Science Fiction & Fantasy Writers of America (SFWA) Website

Adams recommends that potential writers, editors, and agents visit *SFWA.org*,* which has a variety of resources, including guides to getting published, warnings about predatory publishers and agents, and excellent advice for new writers.

*Note: SWFA is a professional organization. Although most of the website is available to the public, the rest is gated to members only. To be admitted, you must qualify by publishing or editing professionally. (See *SFWA.org* for more information.)

If You Want to Write

Consider starting your career writing short stories, rather than novels. It comes down to math. A novel is 80,000 words while a short story averages 5,000 words.

Adams says, "It's easier to level yourself up as a writer with short stories, because you can try and fail over and over, in the span of time that it would take you to just do that once with a novel."

If You Want to Work in Publishing but Without the Starter Salary . . .

According to Adams, "There are other avenues that you could pursue" if you want to earn more money than an editorial assistant. Look into jobs as an agent or a publicist, or work in the advertising department of a publisher. Adams says the experience may help you "transition to a job in publishing where you wouldn't have to start at the bottom."

Here is some other advice to consider.

Take Classes

Because practice makes perfect when it comes to writing and editing, the best place to learn is by doing. Writers will learn that assignments stretch writing muscles you never knew you had, while editors will learn how to provide constructive feedback to help writers write their best.

Join a Writer's Workshop

Science fiction, fantasy, and horror have several excellent writer's workshops that help you hone your talents. Some—such as Clarion, Clarion West, Odyssey—require you to live six weeks at a university campus. These workshops are expensive, but they're taught by successful authors who intimately know their craft. Other workshops are more informal, fan-run affairs held in the evenings or weekends by people who have day jobs and other time commitments.

You may need to polish your writing skills before you apply, as some workshops require you to submit a sample of your work as an "audition" piece.

VOLUNTEER

"Volunteering" is another way of saying "work for free." But volunteering at a publication can provide fodder for your resume, as well as valuable work experience.

Find a small publication that you enjoy, and reach out to the editor. They may put you to work mailing contributor's copies, or perhaps you'll be reading short stories to help find the best ones for your publication.

Volunteering also allows you to learn definitively if the world of publishing is right for you and where you best fit into it.

TURN YOUR FANFIC INTO CASH

You can write about the adventures of Wolverine and his boyfriend Nightcrawler as often as the urge for mutant hook-ups strikes you. But you can't monetize your writing because the characters belong to Marvel.

Fans have found a way around this by writing about the characters of their dreams and removing copyrightable elements. In the case of Wolverine, he's a Canadian with berserker rages and either adamantium or bone claws; in the case of Nightcrawler, he's a blue-furred former German circus performer with the ability to teleport. Clever fanfic writers center their stories on basic characteristics more than super-powered abilities—say, a story featuring the angry, burly logger John and his hirsute, ballet-dancing boyfriend Hans.

E.L. James famously wrote *Fifty Shades of Grey* by using Stephanie Meyer's *Twilight* as a jumping-off point. She wasn't the first person to repackage her fanfic as romance, nor will she be the last.

(TRY TO) PUBLISH YOUR WRITING

Submit your works to magazine and book publishers, and incorporate feedback into your work. You will likely be rejected multiple times—dozens, even—but you will learn what an editor does and does not like about your work. Eventually, you may find yourself with a publishing credit to your name.

If you don't want to spend the long months it takes getting a single story published, consider posting your work online, where readers can find you. (You can place your work on your own site or a platform like Wattpad.)

Then there's the self-publishing route. Authors can self-publish online on sites like Amazon's Kindle Direct Publishing, as well as in print, thanks to options like Lulu, IngramSpark, and others. When you self-publish, you keep the profits for yourself . . . as well as the responsibility and expense of advertising and promoting your work.

GAMING

The world of videogames is a multibillion-dollar business. In 2019 its revenue in the U.S. alone was $35.4 billion (*https://screenrant.com*). The industry's almost 2,500 companies employed 220,000 people (*https://venturebeat.com*). Best of all, the salaries provide a decent standard of living. According to the International Game Developer's Association Developer Satisfaction Survey of 2019, "Most employees (65%) made over $50K USD per year, with the most common salaries being between $50K and $75K USD per year (17%) or between $75K and $100K USD per year (17%)" [survey provided by Sonia Michaels].

Indie game companies, which range from two-person shops to small teams, are also potential sources of employment. Potentially lucrative too. Games like *Stardew Valley* have earned tens of millions of dollars. And then there's *Minecraft*, which indie developer Mojang sold to Microsoft for <reaches for smelling salts> $2.5 billion.

Board games, with their lower barrier to entry—no technical or even interpersonal skills required—may not be as lucrative. But in this industry people can and do make a living. As reported in "Games Broke Funding Records on Kickstarter in 2020, Despite the Pandemic," on Kickstarter alone, board games earned $176.3 million in 2019 and $233 million in 2020 <reaches for the *Wall Street Journal*> (*www.polygon.com*).

There could be a job in there for you somewhere in the gaming industry, right? Quite possibly, if you follow these tips.

Sonia Michaels, DigiPen Institute of Technology

Sonia Michaels (*www.linkedin.com*), who teaches communications and career development at DigiPen Institute of Technology, has helped hundreds of students launch their game industry careers.

If you want a job, you're going to have to work for it—in different locations. The videogame industry is notoriously unstable, and after you've launched your current digital masterpiece, you may be thanked for your hard work by being laid off. Although your present job is in, say, California, your next one could be in Maryland. And let's not forget crunch time, the long hours you need to log as your release date approaches.

Still excited about the idea of creating the painterly images of Hyrule or designing nefarious puzzles that frenzy gamers with frustration? Michaels has the following advice for you.

Know What Kind of Job You Want

If you know how to draw or to code, you already know how to fit in with a games company. But other jobs for wannabe games developers to aim their sights on don't require as much know-how. Michaels says, "If you're really good at organization, communication, and getting people on the same page, you might be a producer. . . . Do research up front to figure out what you're good at, what kind of problems you like to solve, and how much you're willing to learn in the way of hard skills."

Narrow Your Focus

Go to the hiring page of a company you admire, see what skills they're looking for, then work backward. Michaels suggests that if your dream company works with the Unreal game engine, rather than Unity, you should develop your Unreal skills. If your dream job requires C++, start compiling. "And remember to keep your skills current by working on personal projects and/or portfolio pieces," she says.

Go Big or Go Small?

Michaels says that you should know if you prefer to work in a large team or if you prefer to work independently, with more creative control. "Some people are very content to have a small piece of the project that is just theirs," she says. "Maybe they're just doing the art for the running shoes for the NBA game. Other people thrive on more creative input."

It's important to ask yourself this question "before you start casting your net out there," she says. "Otherwise you're going to randomly apply to 200 companies, maybe 150 of which you wouldn't be happy working for."

Make Connections

Considering over 220,000 people are employed in the videogames industry, it's actually a small world. Michaels says, "The videogame industry is only two degrees of separation. If you want to talk to somebody who works at a particular company or in a particular role, if I don't have that information for you, I can reach out to one friend. That information is one person away. That's how small [the industry] is."

Because of this, Michaels says it's important to build connections. "Find people to talk to who are doing the job so that you can find out what it really involves. Follow people on Twitter who are in game production."

Introduce yourself to people in the industry, and "nurture those connections," she says. "Over time check in with people. If you see that they've achieved something, write them a little note of congratulations. If you have a specific question, reach out to them. If something cool happens for you, send them an update."

The industry has a long memory too. "This means you have to be on your best behavior," says Michaels.

ATTEND EVENTS

Go where the game makers are. Developer conferences include Game Developers Conference, SIGGRAPH, and Lightbox, as well as Develop:BrightonDigital in the UK and GCAP in Australia.

To meet people locally, you can attend game jams—where developers create a simple game over a long weekend—and game meetups. (No jams or meetups in your area? Start them yourself and become your area's go-to gal/guy of games.)

HOW COVID-19 HAS HELPED YOU GET A JOB IN THE GAMES INDUSTRY

Michaels says, "Because of the pandemic, industry conferences have gone online, and many of these lectures are available for free. This has been great for expanding accessibility and broadening access."

DEVELOP YOUR PORTFOLIO

Michaels says, "One of the positives about the industry is that it [doesn't require] a bachelor's degree." You just need to prove you can do the work. Create samples and clips to show off what you can bring to your company of choice. This means

Artists should have a portfolio of art.

Programmers should have code samples.

Designers should make their own levels using level editors from existing games.

Writers should teach themselves Twine, to write branching narratives.

Producers should describe how they manage a life cycle of a project, with charts to back up their words.

KNOW THAT YOU MIGHT NOT STAY IN THE JOB YOU STARTED

Another bonus of the games industry, according to Michaels, is "it's less linear than most businesses. You can go from associate producer to engineer or artist. And depending on the size of a company, sometimes you have to wear five hats at a time, and you find that one of those hats suits you better.

"I know one person who started out testing games, and now he's in a management role on the Minecraft team. He's been a designer. He's been a studio head. He's been a producer. And he got laid off like six times from different companies. And every time he got laid off, he trained himself up in something else, and he just kept broadening his experience and skill base," Michaels says. "He talks to my students every semester about using layoffs as a forcing function to keep your career going forward."

KNOW THAT THERE ISN'T MUCH STABILITY

"The crunch-to-contraction cycle is a very real thing and very painful," says Michaels. "There are some employers that will just staff up like crazy, work [their employees] one hundred hours a week, and then lay them off the week after launch. That's why so many developers burn out in six, seven years. . . . This is, of course, terrible in terms of labor practices. I think the industry is struggling really hard to find a way forward through that."

Michaels is guiding students toward the idea that they don't need to accept the current working model of the games industry. "I want [my students] prepared to make those changes, because there's a lot of change that needs to happen in the game industry for it to be a healthy place for people to work. As the new generation of developers moves up, committed to changing things for the better, change will happen."

MUSIC AND PODCASTING

Geek-centered music is not new, nor is monetizing it; filkers (i.e., nerd folk music) The DeHorn Crew sold their tapes (tapes!) at conventions as far back as 1976. Geeky musicians of all genres can find a fanbase in filk, nerdcore, geek rock, and more.

With digital studios like GarageBand, Cubase, Groovepad, and many more, it's easy for musicians to start music-ing. Add the availability of online music stores such as iTunes, Google Play Store, Amazon Music, and Bandcamp, not to mention SoundCloud, Audiomack, Hearthis, and more, coupled with ease of purchase, it's simpler than ever for geeky musicians to monetize their music.

According to Billboard, the U.S. music industry was worth $11.1 billion in 2019, seventy-nine percent from streaming alone (*www.billboard.com*). That's a whole lot of money on the table, waiting for a breakout geek artist.

The audio realm isn't limited to music. Radio plays may not be as popular as they were from 1920 to 1962, a.k.a. the Golden Age of Radio, but radio dramatists can entertain fans on a fraction of the budget of filmmakers.

Podcasting is currently enjoying phenomenal success, providing entertaining, informative verbiage on a multiverse-wide array of topics. The industry was worth $479 million in 2018. That number should be $1 billion in 2021, according to the article "Big Money Is Pouring Into Podcasting. Some Podcasters Love It—But Others Are Freaked Out" (*https://time.com*).

Podcaster jobs are available, typically an established business that wants greater outreach, but they're usually temporary gigs. Full-time employment as a podcaster is as rare as a full suit of beskar armor. If you want a full-time job as a podcaster for a business, creating your own podcast is not bad advice, because in order to get a podcasting job, you'll need to prove your experience . . . with a podcast.

Comic Books

Comic books create galaxy-spanning adventures for the visually inclined, and its characters have become cultural touchstones, particularly in the last twenty years. But they're not an inexpensive pleasure. As anyone who has looked on the upper left-hand corner of their monthly comic book knows, your monthly comic book budget can add up. As of August 2020, issues average $4.41 each (see "Monthly Comic Book Cover Prices" at *www.comichron.com*).

Thanks to fans who absolutely, positively need to know what the Mobius Chair meant when it said there were three Jokers, the industry was worth $1.21 billion in 2019. Of this $1.21 billion, individual comic books accounted for $355 million, and digital comics brought in $90 million. The stand-out sellers of the comic book industry are graphic novels, which earned $765 million, as reported in "Comic Book Sales Recorded an All-Time High in 2019" (*www.cbr.com*). There's a potential reason why graphic novels sold so well: Graphic novels weren't just sold out of your local comic shop; they were also sold from bookstores. According to ComicChron, Diamond Comic Distributors, in 2019 comic book, graphic novel, and magazine sales totaled $529.66 million (see "2019 Comic

Book Sales to Comic Shops" at *https://comichron.com*). But those numbers took a hit to its adamantium jaw due to COVID-19.

With the economic downturn of 2020, there have been layoffs at even the biggest geek businesses, including a culling at DC Comics. This too shall pass. As the blood baths of the mid-1990s have proven, the comic book industry has survived mass layoffs before and has grown back bigger and better.

Meanwhile . . . many of us would love to be a part of the comic book industry; after all, it's where our heroes live. It's about as simple as leaping tall buildings in a single bound.

PAUL LEVITZ

It's harder to get a job in comic books than you would think, according to Paul Levitz (*https://paullevitz.com*), former president of DC Comics. That's because the industry is small, and the number of available jobs even smaller. Levitz says that most of the hirees in a company like DC Comics are "production workers, who . . . basically manag[e] the physical production process and the classic staff functions, accounting, sales, and marketing." Larger companies have a licensing department and an HR department.

Here's the kicker: "There are no staff salary jobs for writers and artists in comics in America."

Yes, you read that right.

"Occasionally," Levitz says, "you'll have a freelancer who does so much work for a single company so well that they'll set up a quasi-salaried arrangement." These exclusive contracts can run for five years. But for the most part, comic book companies work only with freelance writers and artists.

So how can you become one of those exclusively contracted freelancers, who can expect a steady paycheck long enough to lull a landlord into complacency?

Attend Conventions

Some conventions offer portfolio reviews by comic book publishers looking for the next new talent. In five or ten minutes, your work—and the work of everyone else with a portfolio and a love of Jack Kirby—will be assessed by a professional and given constructive criticism. Once in a great while, a talented artist will be asked to submit their art, which could lead to an assignment. Levitz points out that big companies like Marvel or DC may look only at your professional, printed work, "but unpublished stuff, they will not."

Dive into the World of Comic Books

You need to speak intelligently about comic books. "Work in one of the better comic shops that have connections to the freelancers," advises Levitz.

Another way to embed yourself in the world of comics is to write about it. Levitz says, "Twenty years ago, Gail Simone was a hairdresser who wrote an interesting article titled 'Women in Refrigerators,' talking about the mistreatment of women in superhero comics. She'd never written anything professionally in her life, I believe, at that time. But it was a smart enough article that people called her up and said, 'So, Smart Lady, let's see what you can do.' And she became a major writer in the field."

Publish Your Work Online

Levitz also recommends that you post your own comics regularly on your own website. By putting out your own work on a schedule, you're developing a track record. Editors will appreciatively note that you can keep a deadline. He says that publishing your own work not only gives you the opportunity to be noticed but also allows you to monetize your work through platforms like Patreon [see "Patreon," p. 117.].

PUBLISH YOUR WORK IN PRINT

You don't need a publisher to print and sell your own comic. A comic book printer, such as Ka-Blam, Mixam, and PrintNinja, will print your issues or graphic novels, while a distributor, such as Diamond Comic Distributors, will solicit orders from comic and bookstores on your behalf.

The catch, according to Levitz, is that "Comic store owners may or may not order any." Worse, comics are ordered on a nonreturnable basis. If your work doesn't sell, it could easily end up being used for Krypto the Superdog's house training.

Still, having your own comic book is a good way for the dominant publishers to notice you. "It's much easier for an editor to read a printed comic and take it seriously than it is to read a script," says Levitz.

No, you won't get to draw Superman. But maybe you'll get to take Krypto the Superdog out for a walk.

GET YOUR WORK NOTICED

Levitz says, "You can publish comics yourself by going on the web through Webtoons, Amazon [Kindle Direct Publishing], or ComiXology Originals. If you put stuff up and it's good, maybe an editor notices," he says.

For example, Jeff Kinney posted his cartoons to FunBrain, where it grew into a success. The *Diary of a Wimpy Kid* series currently consists of twenty-one books and four films.

Of course, it's up to you to draw readers to your work. Levitz says, "If you're an artist with a rich, sympathetic, significant other, a trust fund, or a parent, you can hire a publicist. For a few thousand bucks, they'll get you interviews in the various media that cover comics. Or you can contact every website, every podcast, yourself."

Get Yourself Noticed

Levitz says, "Go places where people can find you." For example, take classes that have comic book professionals as teachers or guest speakers. "Ask intelligent questions. Go up afterwards, get their card, beg them for an internship. Don't worry about whether you get paid or not."

Then there's word of mouth. Levitz once hired someone because a friend had recommended her. She's now a comic book professional.

What Levitz's advice boils down to: "Put yourself where somebody can find you."

And the Best Way to Get Yourself Noticed Is . . .

There are only two ways to garner attention in the comic book industry, according to Levitz. "Be brilliant or be lucky. . . . Being brilliant works much better."

LESSONS LEARNED

Every business has problems, hitches, growing pains, and outright disasters. In some cases, these errors can be avoided. In others, there's nothing you can do except work through them as best as you can. If you learn from these ahead of time, you'll be able to avoid them. Don't worry . . . you'll have other mistakes to call your own.

Lesson: The UD Designs warehouse burned down in 2019. Luckily, owner David Pea had insurance. But "over a quarter million dollar's worth of inventory" went up in smoke, he says, including an important piece that had a hard deadline.

Learned: Meet your deadlines, no matter how difficult.

It's important that you keep your promises, and not just because you're contractually obligated: Chris McLennan's show Phoenix FearCon had a terrible financial setback [see the following case study], but because she paid people what she owed them, her personal reputation remains intact. Thus Phoenix FearCon continues to attract industry talent and fans alike.

Also, if your inventory is worth more than you can easily replace, get insurance.

Lesson: SpiderMind Games took months to fulfill the backer rewards of its first Kickstarter—specialized dice—because the manager of the dice company suddenly passed away. "[His death] put the factory in chaos because he controlled pretty much everything to do with the production," says SpiderMind producer Jon Lunn. These dice were so special that many backers asked for a refund, rather than have the Kickstarted game without it.

Learned: Keep your rewards "relatively straightforward," says Lunn. (See "Simplify Your Backer Rewards Even More," p. 115.) And that means no unique items . . . at least, not without a contingency plan.

Lesson: At one show where Tea & Absinthe boothed, potential customers said that, although they would have loved to buy tea, they couldn't because of the high price of their VIP tickets. "This particular show was all about extracting money from people before they even got there," says co-owner Daniel Myers. And he hadn't realized it until the doors opened.

If you fail to make a profit at a convention, most people would chalk it up to "It's just the way the fish fingers crumble." But Myers says if business fails to earn a healthy profit, it's his fault because, "We didn't do our homework."

Learned: Do your research, and speak to fellow geektrepreneurs about the experiences they had at a convention you're considering.

Now that he has enough experience, Myers knows which kind of convention works best for Tea & Absinthe, and he avoids the rest.

Lesson: Not having a lawyer review your contract.

Learned: See below.

Case Study: How Chris McLennan's Phoenix FearCon Lost $115,000

Chris McLennan has a full-time job and a semi-permanent side hustle. "I had always put on shows: comedy shows, wrestling shows, burlesque shows, belly dance shows, all kinds."

Meanwhile, her husband runs the pop culture zine TrashCity.org. McLennan attended film festivals with him . . . and they bored her completely. She envisioned an alternative film festival, one more like a convention, with musical guests and free-roaming cosplaying zombies. She staged the first Phoenix FearCon at a friend's art gallery. Fans showed up for the films, the one celebrity who attended, and the bar. The event was a success, and she expanded into a local movie theater, where her convention ran for three years.

Disaster struck in 2014. McLennan had rented a site for her first weekend-long event, a large plot of land that also held several haunted mansions for attendees to explore. The owner offered her a weekend when the site would otherwise be closed. She signed a contract.

"But then he partnered up with another haunt, who told him that they had to stay open, including the dates of my event," says McLennan. She couldn't cancel because, "Our contract didn't say specifically that the place would be closed on those days."

The result: Although Phoenix FearCon had its own entrance, the scary mansion tour kept the main entrance open—where it collected the entrance fee of every attendee, including the ones who were there for Phoenix FearCon. The owners of the haunted house site, McLennan says, "kept all the money that went through the door.

"We were out of pocket $115,000. We ended up taking a mortgage out on our house to make up for all that money that we paid out." Legally, she had no recourse, as her contract didn't specify that Phoenix FearCon would have the site to itself.

With that, McLennan offers the following advice: "Make sure that your contracts are set in stone with the exact details of what it is that you expect. Make sure that you don't fall into this situation like we did." says McLennan. "Because I knew the owner of the haunt for so many years, I kind of let my guard down. Of course, the last thing I expected was the exact thing that happened."

Subsequent Phoenix FearCons have continued to earn a profit.

Lesson: Through no fault of your own, a company can move on without you.
Learned: See below.

Case Study: ThinkGeek's Jennifer Frazier Gets Fired from the $140 Million Company She Cofounded

ThinkGeek sold geeky goods at all price points from its online store, and this eclectic blend of merchandise was beloved by fans. The ThinkGeek team (Willie Vadnais, Scott Smith, Jon Sime, and Jennifer Frazier) hadn't started out to become an online convention's dealer's room. Actually, they started out as WizardNet, a dial-up internet service provider.

Frazier, one of ThinkGeek's cofounders, says, "WizardNet was using free and open source software, and the community supports each other. Willie recognized the value of this unsung group of heroes that were keeping the internet running. He said, 'Wouldn't it be cool to have fun stuff and merchandise to celebrate them?'"

At that time, in August 1999, few other companies were dedicated to geeky merch. It was clear there was a market: "It took us several years to be profitable, but we were making money right away."

After one month and one good review on then-geeky authority Slashdot, ThinkGeek's servers crashed. Frazier says, "We thought, 'This is great. Crap, what are we going to do?'" They managed by putting a lot of sweat into their sweat equity. "We answered the phones and email. We drove all hours to our T-shirt supplier in terrible traffic. We stayed up late packing orders, and we shipped boxes in midnight runs. We did it all."

"Around the same time, Slashdot was acquired by Andover.net, and [someone at] Slashdot told Andover, 'Hey, you should buy ThinkGeek.'" Frazier says, "We sold the business to Andover.net by October."

Let that sink in. The business was acquired *two months* after it was created.

The cofounders were paid in both cash and stock, along with an agreement that the team would stay on and run the business, which was later acquired by VA Linux Systems. Frazier was in charge of company culture and helped create "fun, uplifting products" that made people "be proud to be a geek." Merch included a tauntaun sleeping bag; a bag of holding; and tea, Earl Grey.

The company grew to eighty-three employees. In 2011, its revenue was $118.9 million.

In 2012, Frazier was laid off.

By that time, the parent company, then known as Geeknet, had "lots of corporate involvement, and executives benefited financially from this hard work and a piece of our souls that went into this business." She describes the 2012 version of ThinkGeek as a place that was willing to "sell products that would make us more money but not really fit the idea of what a geek should be."

So how does it feel to get fired from the job you created?

"It feels like shit," Frazier says. But she brings what she learned about online retail to her current job as the Director of Jewelry Merchandising of the geektastic MiniMuseum.

Videogame retail store GameStop ultimately purchased ThinkGeek in 2015 for $140 million. Although GameStop owns ThinkGeek, it does little to promote the ThinkGeek brand. At the time of writing, GameStop has no mention of ThinkGeek on its website.

Closing Down

You may have had some success in your geek business—but not enough to make it worth your time. You may even have had a reasonable amount of success, but real life has reared its less-than-lovely head. You may have to shut down your geeky business.

Good news: When you create your business, you're given a unique employer identification number (EIN), which is never reused. This means you can always restart your business at any time; of course, take a look at the circumstances that led you to shut it in the first place so that you don't repeat any mistakes.

Here's how to close down your business.

Consult a Lawyer or Financial Professional in Your State

Remember that state laws vary, so be sure to consult a lawyer or financial professional as necessary.

File a Final Return

The type of corporation structure you have, say, an LLC, determines the type of tax return you file. While some states require that you fill out all of the forms you did when you first started your venture, other states will make you sign only one or two.

Pay Your Employees and Contract Workers

Although many of you won't have employees, some of you may. Pay them for the work they've done. Remember to give them their W-2 forms too.

If you hired a freelancer during the calendar year, and you paid them more than $600, you'll have to give them a 1099 form, as well as report their earnings to the U.S. government with a 1096 form.

Pay Your Taxes

Just because your business is no longer operating, that doesn't mean you won't owe taxes for the months that it was. If you had employees, you'll also be subject to employment tax. Pay up, 'cuz tax evasion won't impress anyone in the yard.

Cancel Your EIN

Send a letter to the IRS, stating that you're closing your business. This step is important, because as the IRS writes on the "Closing a Business Page" on its website, "We cannot close your business account until you have filed all necessary returns and paid all taxes owed" (*www.irs.gov*). The IRS also wants you to provide a reason for your closing your business, likely for data-gathering purposes.

Hang On to Your Records

Keep employment records for four years. If you claim losses, the IRS recommends you keep them for seven.

Dispose of Inventory

Unless you plan a quick comeback, sell your equipment so that other makers can put it to good use. There will be tax implications, so set aside a portion of your sales to make good during tax time.

Take Emotional Stock

Now that you've closed your business, take time to clear your head, and even to mourn, if you need to. This work could have been simply something for you to do to make a few bucks on weekends. Or perhaps it was your pride and joy, the reason you loved what you did. What inspired you will always be there. Now do something else differently wonderful with your life.

Six Not-So-Secret Secrets to Business Success

Throughout the interviews for this book, multiple interviewees shared what made them successful. While their businesses were as different as their inspirations, their success had several facets in common.

Be at the Right Time and Place

Online shop ThinkGeek sold geeky goods back in 1999, when there were few online sellers in the geek space at that time. This shop carved itself a market worth over $100 million.

Chris McLennan didn't put much advertising into her convention Phoenix FearCon, but attendance grew from 85 to a respectable 2,000 in one year. But attendance leapt to 16,000 attendees after *The Walking Dead* premiered, and Phoenix FearCon captured the zombie zeitgeist.

As Etsy sewers and makers learned during the pandemic, when the public required face masks, the best way to be a business at the right time is to *have* a business when the right time happens.

Go Where No Business Has Gone Before

Catherine Elhoffer makes sweaters and knitwear for the geeky crowd. As there are few other geek clothiers in the knitwear space, Elhoffer Designs stands out. Elhoffer was also one of the first geeky designers to identify and capitalize on the market for higher-end clothing in the geek space.

Lean on Your Previous Education and Experience

Reece Robbins had something that set Frontline Gaming ahead of the pack of new businesses. As a freelance writer who had written about gaming, "I established a name by producing quality content on a regular basis. It was pretty easy to leverage that into creating our own blog."

Be Talented and Creative

Many successful geektrepreneurs are preternaturally talented with imagination to boot. Having next-level skills does not guarantee success. But it certainly helps.

Have More Than One Income Stream

While some geektrepreneurs work full- or part-time jobs to help pay the rent, others create parallel income streams. Making geeky T-shirts *and* taking commissions. Developing board- or videogames *and* teaching classes on game development. Creating jewelry *and* editing videos for a jewelry-making YouTube channel. Podcasting *and* writing.

Keep Your Friends Close

To repeat from chapter 1: even if you do all of the work, you will still benefit from the people around you. The friends who play-test your game. The spouse who edits your writing. And most important of all, the fans who share your passion and want to buy what you're selling because you offer exactly what they want that they're not getting anywhere else.

Jon Lunn says that Spidermind Games wouldn't have succeeded without the help of the community. "I spent a lot of my time reaching out to people, and it's amazing how many people in the industry, people who've just set themselves up, are willing to help. There have been so many people who are incredibly kind and happy to offer their advice. Don't be afraid to ask."

Nor would this book exist without the countless interviewees who selflessly gave their time and hard-earned acumen. Help, if you need it, can be a phone call or DM away. Fandom is a virtuous circle. And that's our superpower.

GEEK-CENTERED WORK

If you're generally creative but have no compass, here are some of the ways geeky people have earned money, some of them unique to the geekosphere.

MICRO-INFLUENCING

In 2015, Emma Lambert's husband and friend created WebDM, a Dungeons & Dragons-themed YouTube channel. In 2017, they attended a convention together, where the WebDM team was surrounded by fans. That's when Lambert suddenly realized that they were influencers. She soon sought to monetize this. Here's how she turned influencing into secondary income.

ASK FOR SPONSORSHIP

At conventions, Lambert says, "I spend all of my time on the expo floor talking about WebDM to people who had booths. I give them my card, I would try to get theirs, and then I would follow up with them."

This way, Lambert was able to select the sponsors she wanted, specifically, those who were on brand. This leads to . . .

ACCEPT ONLY SPONSORS WHO ARE ON BRAND

Lambert accepts sponsorships only from businesses that are on brand. Because she accepts on-brand sponsors, her viewers remain immersed in the world of gaming, whether they see ads relating to *the game* (as with the D&D spells company Ink & Lyre) or relating to *gamers* (as with Audible.com, who let Lambert recommend books she thought WebDM fans would enjoy.)

"The goal is really to connect with people," Lambert says. "It's not necessarily about how to sell to them."

ACCEPT SPONSORSHIP ONLY FROM BRANDS YOU LIKE

Lambert says, "We work with brands who offer products that we like and would actually use." She believes that endorsing a product is "a responsibility."

Your fans trust you to recommend products to them. To keep that trust, don't take money from a company you wouldn't promote without the money. Lambert says, "I don't want to do anything that will jeopardize our connection with our audience."

KNOW WHAT TO CHARGE

Here's where the data comes in. (And Lambert says she's "very data driven.") Online research suggests a simple formula, such as a flat rate, divided by the number of thousand followers you have. It looks like this:

If you have 1,000 followers, you might consider charging $10.

If you have 10,000 followers, you could charge $100.

If you have 53,298 followers, you can charge $532.98. Et cetera.

With a following of under 200,000 (at the time of writing), Lambert charges $1,200 per sponsorship post. She recalculates that number monthly. Lambert says, "Creators typically charge a rate anywhere between $8 to $30 per thousand views/downloads/engagements." She charges more for YouTube sponsorship, a platform that has high production value, and less for podcast sponsorship.

But First, Test What You Charge

Lambert "lowballed" her first sponsors, that is, undercharged them, because she was genuinely unsure what the results would be. When her sponsors shared their data with her, she found that WebDM's mentions were successful. From this, she said, "I could build a record of return." When Lambert says she believes a sponsorship will yield certain results, she has the data to back her claim. "It's important to me that that's the truth."

The U.S. Laws Surrounding Influencing

The Federal Trade Commission has rules concerning what influencers can and cannot say, to protect consumers against predatory sales tactics. If you're in violation of these rules, it will nuke your wallet from orbit.

You must reveal that you received an item for free (if you paid for it, no disclosure necessary).

You must disclose the relationship you have with the makers of the product/services you're recommending.

You must tell the truth. Even if you dislike the item.

You must actually try the product that you're talking about.

You must use appropriate disclosures, depending on the type of social media you use:

- On Twitter and Facebook, state that you were given a product for free by using appropriate hashtags, such as #sponsored #ad #paid.

- On YouTube, mention the sponsorship at the beginning of your video.

- On SnapChat or Instagram/Facebook stories, superimpose your disclosure over your images.

- On a live stream, mention your sponsor several times, so people who tune in at various points know you're being sponsored.

- Consult a lawyer.

For more information, see *https://ftc.gov/influencers*.

Cosplaying for Dollars

Cosplayers have been attending conventions since there have been conventions . . . back in 1939. Cosplayers rarely make enough money to support themselves. But you absolutely can support your Worbla habit.

Ash Miller, who has been cosplaying since 2015, advises, "My biggest advice to people who want to monetize cosplay is that you have to be social, to put yourself out there, and make connections, even though it's scary. Because you could be doing the best work in the whole entire world, but if no one knows you're doing it, no one's gonna want to pay you for it."

Further advice comes from cosplayers Tiffani Daniel and Sarah Harman. Here are eight ways that people who dress up as their favorite characters—or even as the carpet from their favorite hotel—can earn money.

ATTEND CONVENTIONS

If you're a cosplayer with your own following, conventions may pay you to attend. Body-positive cosplayer Miller says she's received "anywhere from $50 and covering transportation to a couple hundred [dollars]."

Conventions also compensate cosplayers in other ways. "You may not get paid," Miller says, "but you will get a free table and an opportunity to sell yourself and your things." (Miller formerly sold her handmade jewelry.)

HOST "CHARACTER PARTIES"

Miller also earns money at "character parties," where she entertains children dressed as a character not of her own creation. "My advertising is word of mouth," she says. Whenever she attends one party, other attendees will ask for her card. Miller, who has a full-time job, believes she could get more party jobs if she advertised. If you do advertise, she warns, be careful of how you position yourself. "You have to steer away from [IP-infringing] language, especially when you're signing a contract."

SELL PHOTOS

At conventions, Miller sells pictures of herself in various cosplay regalia in 4" × 6" photos, 8" × 10" photos, and postcards. Miller works with professional photographers and pays them for the rights to use her photos. Sometimes, they will give her her rights for free; on rare occasions, she splits the profits of her sales. Then she has the photos printed via Sharp Prints.

WORK AS AN INFLUENCER

Daniel says that cosplayers can make money as influencers for brands that they use and appreciate. [See "The U.S. Laws Surrounding Influencing" on pp. 187–188.] Daniel reaches out to brands by mailing them her media kit. [See p. 191.] For her work posting a few images to Instagram or discussing a product on YouTube, she has charged up to $300.

If you don't think you have a large enough following to begin influencing, think again: Daniel started early in her cosplaying career, where she had merely "one thousand [Instagram] followers and essentially no presence anywhere."

TAKE SEWING COMMISSIONS

Taking sewing commissions is "really a great option" for the cosplayer who wants to earn money, says Daniel. You need to know how to manage your time, as well as manage the expectations of a client who might not know how long it takes to make a garment. Daniel says that many cosplaying sewers post their work on Etsy.

CREATE EBOOKS AND PATTERNS

Daniel recommends that you teach others your hard-earned knowledge by selling an ebook for cosplayers. If you've created sewing patterns for a popular character or a guide to building cosplay props, you can sell that too.

THROW A COSPLAY EVENT

Harman earns a small amount of money throwing a "Cosplay Prom," an annual event that marries a fabulous party with formal versions of cosplay favorites. Her event, held in Dallas, Texas, even offers prizes to the Prom King and Prom Queen, as well as the occasional door prize for attendees.

SELL YOUR OLD COSTUMES

Have your sewing skills improved to the point where your older costumes no longer spark joy? Sell your older pieces, and give someone else a chance to enjoy them.

BONUS OPTION: GET A FULL-TIME JOB

A small pool of very talented (and lucky) cosplayers have been hired by the companies whose characters they've recreated. These cosplay gigs, which include events and in-person appearances, are few and far between. For the ones who achieve it, it's a cosplay dream come true (see "What It's Like to Cosplay for Money" at *https://cosplay.kotaku.com*).

CREATE A MEDIA KIT

To pique the interest of a convention or to attract sponsors, create a media kit. A media "kit"—formerly a set of promotional materials meant for the press—is simply one or two pages of facts: who you are, your social media reach, the services you provide to clients, and any awards and links to press coverage, with images if relevant (such as cosplayers).

As an example, here is a media kit that has landed paid appearances, courtesy of cosplayer Tiffani Daniel.

cosplay & coffee

 cosplayer.

writer.

 host.

 coffee fiend.

TIFFANI AKA
COSPLAY AND COFFEE

WRITER AND COSPLAYER

A writer turned cosplayer, Tiffani started cosplayandcoffee.com to write about the cosplay community. She has conducted several cosplayer and celebrity interviews for her YouTube channel, Cosplay and Coffee.

Tiffani is recognized for many of her cosplays as well as her writing on websites such as Screen Rant.

COSPLAYAND
COFFEE.COM

COSPLAY
AND
COFFEE

@COSPLAYAND
COFFEE

@COSPLAYN
COFFEE

@COSPLAYN
COFFEE

TIFFANIDANIELCC@GMAIL.COM
ORLANDO, FL

AUDIENCE

January 2021

Facebook: 4,700
Twitter: 1,500
Instagram: 7,660
YouTube: 1,140

Website: 4,500 Page Views
Per Month

DEMOGRAPHICS

Women: 44.8%
Men: 55.2%
Age(s): 18-35
Location(s): US, UK, Germany,
Australia, Canada

SPECIALTIES

Tiffani is an entertainment
journalist of 5 years with bylines
in national publications such as:

Screen Rant
Comic Book Resources
Inside the Magic
Movie Pilot

POPULAR FEATURES

Website:
Tutorials
Interviews
Convention Coverage

YouTube:
Product Reviews
Interviews/Collaborations

TIFFANIDANIELCC@GMAIL.COM
ORLANDO, FL

CONVENTION SHOWRUNNER

Want to run your own convention? Spat Oktan offers advice to people who like conventions and thrive on adrenaline [see "Case Study: Spat Oktan Accidentally Becomes a Convention Showrunner," p. 137.].

THERE'S NO SUCH THING AS A REAL JOB DESCRIPTION

You will be required to wear multiple hats, no matter how unglamorous, frequently at the same time. Oktan's work includes

- Organizing dealer's rooms and the artist alley
- Assigning each and every volunteer a job
- Recruiting celebrity guests
- Protecting celebrity guests from creepy fans
- Picking up trash from the convention floor
- Tricking celebrity guests into judging a costume competition
- Placating irate celebrity guests who have been tricked into judging a competition

RECOGNIZE THAT BEING A FAN CAN BE A DETRIMENT

"Being a fan is important and a hindrance at the same time," says Oktan. If you're a fan, you know what appeals to geekdom. But as a fan, you may have an attachment to a show or an actor that only a few share. If you spend your budget paying to fly in actors that no one turns out to see, then the convention loses.

Then there's saying no to actors whom you personally enjoy. Oktan says, "There's one actor who I love to death. But I don't want to book [him], because every third convention, he destroys the hotel room in some kind of drunken rampage."

You Have to Choose the Right Staff

Oktan learned that not every volunteer was there to help; they were there to meet their own geek heroes, then suddenly disappear. As a showrunner, you need to develop a sense of who has staying power. Oktan advises that you find the right volunteers, train them . . . then trust them to do their jobs.

Be Good to Your Volunteers

Even though volunteers are unpaid, Oktan tries to compensate them when he can. Although he can't guarantee it, "I try to put together a swag bag for them at the end." His swag bags have included T-shirts or perhaps a few celebrity autographs.

Be Good to the Fans

If Oktan sees a fan has arrived too late for an autograph, he will run to the Green Room, where the guests relax between events, to see if the star is still available. Good showrunners know that conventions are about the fans. Go out of your way to make them happy.

Seen for Sale

Fashion:

Let these current items, experiences, and ephemerals inspire your future business.

T-shirts

Upcycled/remixed T-shirts

Upcycled T-shirts and added skirts

Cosplay-inspired clothes

Clothing made from licensed fabric

Clothing that evokes well-known characters

Polo shirts with licensed characters/unique designs

Decoupaged shoes and purses

Knitware patterns based on board games

Cloth face masks

Accessories:

Lanyards

Weapons

Swords, knives

"Laser swords"

Foam weapons

Blasters

Modded Nerf guns

Jewelry (necklaces, bracelets, earrings, ankle bracelets)

Hair fascinators

Hats

Frames for glasses

Belts/belt buckles

Purses/pouches/wallets/bags/backpacks/messenger bags

Corsets/jerkins

Rubber/foam face masks

Cloisonné/metal pins

PERSONAL CARE:

Makeup

Nail polish/nail art

Perfume

Soap

Candles

COSPLAY:

Making:

Cosplay outfits/pieces

Elf ears

Armor

Shields

Patterns

Props (magic wands, spellbooks, etc.)

Cosplay model

Cosplay photographer

Selling:

Cosplay craft materials (foam, paint, etc.)

Wigs, wig care products, and wig dyes

Fabric

ART:

Creating fine art; paintings

Drawing fans as a superhero/videogame avatar/furry/fantastical version of themselves

Drawing popular characters as steampunk/bombshell/alternative versions of themselves

Creating sculptures and figurines

Painting figurines

Designing/creating 3D printed figurines for either IP holders or for sites like Cults3D, MyMiniFactory, or Shapeways.

Designing/creating 2D .svg files for Cricut and other cutting machines

Creating plush characters

Modding existing dolls

Making stained glass artwork

Making metal art

Designing geeky playing cards/tarot cards

Creating geeky coloring books, filming yourself drawing horror scenes in children's coloring books

Building geeky wall clocks

Building shadowboxes

Sandblasting mugs/beer steins

FILM:

Fan commentary

Fan films

Television/movie breakdowns

Episode overviews

Explanations

Science fiction/fantasy/horror

Documentaries

Film festivals (production)

PUBLISHING:

Small press publishing

Editing (print and online, fiction and nonfiction)

Writing (fiction)

Novels

Short stories/novelettes/novellas

Poetry

Plays

Interactive fiction (via *https://twinery.org*)

Translating non-English science fiction/fantasy works

Writing (nonfiction)

How-to

Culture

Biographies

Articles

Game walkthroughs

Cookbooks

Book agenting

Publicity

Music/Podcasts:

Making music (all genres)

Creating podcasts

Creating radio dramas

Videogames:

Creating AAA videogames

Creating Indie videogames

Creating mods of videogames

Twitch videogame livestreaming

E-sport athlete

Gaming Supplies (Dungeons & Dragons)

Developing board/card/role-playing games

Owning/running board game store

Explaining board games/RPGs on YouTube

Working as a professional dungeon master

Creating/running escape rooms

Creating:

Specialized dice

Dice towers

Dice boxes and bags

Curated spells

Modules

DM screens

Playmats (online and physical)

Dice jewelry

Backpacks/carry bags for board games

Custom meeples

Comic Books

Grading comic books

Selling:

New comic books

Specialized comic collections (horror, Silver Age, Bronze Age, graphic novels only)

Autographed comic books

Certified comic books

Original panels/covers

Plastic comic book covers/cardboard backing

RESELLER:

Reselling previously owned collections:

Toys

Books

Comic books

Autographs

Autographed items

OTHER:

Zombie themed mud-run

Haunted house (seasonal)

Tour guide of geeky film locations

Your own convention/film festival

ABOUT THE AUTHOR

Carol Pinchefsky is a domain expert in all things geek. She has written almost 2,000 articles about geek culture for *SyFy.com*, *Playboy.com*, *Forbes.com*, *GeekandSundry.com*, *PC Gamer*, *Lightspeed* magazine, and *SFX*, as well as technology, science, and business for markets that include the *New York Times*, Hewlett-Packard Enterprise, MacLife, and the blog of the Society for Neuroscience. She won the Newspace Journalism Award in 2012.

She attended Clarion West Writers Workshop in 1995. When not writing, she volunteers with the nonprofit Teachers in Space. She also works as the humor competition editor for *The Magazine of Fantasy & Science Fiction*. Prior to that, she worked as an editor for *The Fast Track*, an associate editor for *SEXLife* magazine, and an editorial assistant for *Weird Tales* magazine.

In addition, she has moderated convention panels, been interviewed on radio and podcasts, and appeared as the judge in a science-fiction–themed episode of *The Food Network Challenge*.

She has seen geek culture grow from a small underground community into a thriving network into a financial powerhouse. She is glad to be a part of it.

She lives with her husband and their books.